The Castle Brom... ...eutenant
Kustrzynski being ... ...ransport-
ation to a scrap dum...

IN ENEMY HANDS

Revealing true stories behind wartime Allied aircraft losses

Bryan Philpott
Foreword by Sir Douglas Bader

PSL Patrick Stephens, Cambridge

Frontispiece *Stirling N3705, coded* MG-F *of 7 Squadron after it fell into German hands whilst experiencing mechanical problems during a mining mission. See* 'A prize for the Luftwaffe' *page 19.*

First published in 1981

British Cataloguing in Publication Data

Philpott, Bryan
   In enemy hands.
    1. Aeronautics—Europe—Accidents
    2. World War, 1939-1945—Aerial operations
    I. Title
    940.54'4   D785

   ISBN 0-85059-499-5

Photoset in 10 pt Plantin by Manuset Limited, Baldock, Herts. Printed in Great Britain on 100 gsm Fineblade coated cartridge, and bound, by The Garden City Press, Letchworth, Herts, for the publishers, Patrick Stephens Limited, Bar Hill, Cambridge, CB3 8EL, England.

Foreword by Group Captain Sir Douglas Bader CBE, DSO★, DFC★.

A great deal of research must have gone into this book. It will be nostalgic for some of those aircrew who were shot down (particularly those who bailed out) to see a picture of their aeroplane taken by the Germans when they collected it and took it away, either for examination if it was in reasonable condition, or for destruction. I feel, therefore, this book will have a ready sale to all those airmen, regardless of which side they were on, who fought in World War 2. It is easy to read and provides great visual interest. I commend it.

(Photo courtesy of the International Air Tattoo.)

Introduction

In recent years it has become fashionable for writers to analyse the tactics and strategy of the air war of 1939-45, and then proceed to attack those responsible for decisions made or even for their conduct.

All of us have perfect hindsight, and no doubt some of the comments made have contained an element of truth. But surely it is not particularly clever, or indeed necessary, to aim criticism at commanders who may now no longer be able to defend themselves, or who were acting on instructions of which they themselves may also have doubted the wisdom but were in no position to query. It is also quite wrong to dismiss the efforts of the aircrew who were set a task and carried it out without question. Such men were volunteers and represented a cross-section of our nation's manhood. They chose to fight their war from the cramped confines of a fighter, the drafty interior of a bomber, or one of the many other types of aircraft which contributed vital and necessary work. Unlike the soldier who, once he went into a combat area, was constantly exposed to danger, or the sailor who faced death from the sky, the sea and the elements, men who flew were often adjusting themselves to widely varying environments. Bomber crews for example operated, in the main, from bases in their own country, where they were surrounded by friends and what creature comforts were available to the civil population. Then came a period of adjustment to facing the dangers of a long flight over hostile territory and the possibility of a violent death, or a lonely parachute descent into an environment which could hold unthinkable terrors. If all went well, it was back to the mess, another party, another drink at the local, perhaps a passing thought or two about a friend who had not returned, and another period of adjustment. In such situations little thought was given to the rights or wrongs of strategic bombing, or aerial warfare—there was a job to be done and the sooner it was over with the better. Perhaps moralising about war, re-fighting it with table-top strategy, and considering aspects that were not known at the time by those taking decisions, is good selling material in today's world where, in many quarters, to protect one's lifestyle, country, and beliefs by providing a strong defence is looked upon as being immoral. Possibly this attitude is good for the ego of the authors concerned and those who like to see popular heroes ridiculed. This book is not for that type of person; nor is it for those who seek justification in war. I have set out to tell the stories of the men, and in some cases the aircraft in which they flew, who four decades ago chose to fight for their country in the air, and for one reason or another, ended 'In enemy hands'. To all of them we owe a great debt which must never be forgotten.

Acknowledgements

The compilation of this book would not have been possible without the help of many people and organisations. Whilst I must accept total responsibility for the final presentation of the text, I could not have even begun to compile it without the raw material so generously supplied through the efforts of the following, whose help is most gratefully acknowledged:

Frau Marriane Loenertz and Dr Haupt of the Bundesarchiv; Major-General John Huston, Major-General James Ahmann, Lieutenant-Colonel James Salminen, Lieutenant-Colonel James Waddell of the USAF; Group Captain Bill Randle, Wing Commander Clifford Phillips, Squadron Leader John Boulter of the Royal Air Force; The Department of General Services and Administration National Archives and Records Service, Washington; The Albert F. Simpson Historical Research Center of the USAF; Maxwell Air Force Base; The Public Records Office, London; The Air Historical Branch MOD; The Independent Television Authority, Southern Television; The Editors of *Air Mail* and the *Air Force Times*; and the following, Alfred Price, Wally Stanton, Michael J.F. Bowyer, Eric Marsden, John Clive who very kindly made available his research into *KG200*, L.C. Ridley, Mike Bailey, Norman Ottaway, Chris Thomas, Roy Lowman, Tony North, Peter Kirk and the German and Allied aircrew who answered my various published appeals. Last but by no means least, my wife Susan, who in the last 18 months must, on many occasions, have wished that World War 2 had never happened, for totally different reasons to those who also share the same sentiment.

About this book

During my research in the photographic department of the Bundesarchiv, for material used in the *World War 2 Photo-Album* series (also published by Patrick Stephens Ltd), I discovered a considerable number of photographs of Allied aircraft which had fallen victim to anti-aircraft guns, fighters or even mechanical problems, as a result of which they had crashed in enemy territory. A large quantity of these photographs was collected and from these the selection now published were researched to the best of my ability. This research resulted in the stories which now accompany them. It has been a very enjoyable task involving considerable correspondence, travel, and much frustration.

Many people interested in aviation have fixed, and often inflexible ideas of air operations, and camouflage and markings, as well as an unshakable belief that official records are always right and must never be queried. I have not set out deliberately to prove that such idealistic thoughts do not come from the genuine expert, but some of the facts revealed will clearly show that attitudes of mind must be flexible if one wishes to be considered a genuine authority on such matters. I am not for one moment attempting to place myself on such a pinnacle, but I do hope that my efforts will help to redress the balance.

The information I have collected has been derived from many sources, and the facts quoted are genuine in the sense that they have been verified wherever possible from different authorities. Weather conditions, combat reports, map co-ordinates, etc, are not figments of my imagination, similarly any crew conversations reported and raid details supplied are genuine and have not been assumed simply to add an air of authenticity. In cases where it proved impossible to trace the true details surrounding a featured aircraft, I have presented the facts as they appear from the photograph and leave the reader to draw his own conclusions.

I very much hope that my efforts will be viewed in the spirit in which I have made them, and I shall be delighted to hear from any reader who can supply any missing details or perhaps unravel some of the secrets which have defeated me.

Important

The photographs in this book are reproduced by kind permission of the Bundesarchiv, Koblenz. We have been asked to stress that copies of these pictures CANNOT be supplied to private collectors but will only be made available to *bona fide* authors and publishers. Anyone wishing to use these pictures should make a request directly to the Bundesarchiv and *not* to Patrick Stephens Limited.

Dedication

This book is dedicated to aircrew of all nations who died in the service of their country.

The Channel Dash

At 23.00 hours on February 11 1942, the battle cruisers *Scharnhorst* and *Gneisenau* together with the heavy cruiser *Prinz Eugen*, slipped their moorings in the French port of Brest and, with an escort of seven destroyers, headed into the English Channel. One of Germany's most daring and successful sea operations was about to begin.

Since early 1941 the three ships had been under constant aerial survey, and their presence in Brest had kept part of the British Home Fleet, as well as units of the Mediterranean Fleet stationed in the Gibraltar area, constantly on their toes waiting for the expected break-out.

The eventual move by the ships was planned to a very fine degree and carried out in utmost secrecy. A vast flotilla of escorts and constant air cover by the Luftwaffe which provided a total of 282 aircraft, gave adequate support as well as underlining the importance to the Germans of the success of the operation. The escape of the ships went unnoticed by the British until they were spotted by a reconnaissance aircraft when they were well under way. Immediately all British forces were alerted and ships of the Royal Navy together with strike aircraft of the Fleet Air Arm and Royal Air Force, set out to attack the German force. Among the units detailed to provide fighter cover for the bombers were 234 and 129 Squadrons.

The Spitfires of 129 (Mysore) Squadron were detailed to provide escort for six cannon-armed Hurricanes of 1 Squadron operating

This page and overleaf *The all black Langley-built Hurricane IIB of Pilot Officer Marcinkus. The aircraft has an RDM 2 black finish and carries an 18-inch diameter type C1 fuselage roundel, which has quite clearly been painted over the former 36-inch diameter marking, the latter possibly being a type A1. The squadron code JX and individual letter J, as well as the serial (BD949) are in red. It is interesting to note the layout of the codes on the starboard fuselage sides, where the individual letter J is carried aft of the roundel, the more common practice being JX-J. Spitfire RY-D, seen in the background of one of the photographs, is a 313 Squadron aircraft and carries the more common 36-inch diameter type A1 roundel between its light grey codes. The port wing of this machine has a 50-inch type A roundel painted on its undersurface.*

8

from Tangmere. The six Hurricanes were called to readiness at 11.40 hours and two hours later the order to embark on what was known as 'Operation Fuller' crackled over the lines to Tangmere. Led by Flight Lieutenant W. Raymond flying Hurricane *Z3970* the six Hurricanes of 'A' Flight headed into the overcast sky to rendezvous with 12 Spitfires from 129 Squadron. Ten minutes into the mission Raymond spotted four destroyers and ordered his six aircraft into battle formation to attack the enemy ships which were steaming in line astern towards the north-east. The Hurricanes swung over the ships and screamed down to low level attacking the destroyers, which were by now throwing up a heavy flak barrage, from the direction of the Belgian coast. Flying at a height of 50 feet the Hurricanes, which were in three sections of two, held their fire until they were less than 100 yards from the ships. White Section consisted of Sergeant E. Blair, a South African, flying *Z3774*, and a Lithuanian pilot, Pilot Officer R. Marcinkus flying *BD949*. Pulling up from his attack and jinking through the flak, Raymond caught sight of a Hurricane erupting in a ball of flame as it was hit by its target's guns. His attention was then concentrated on getting his own aircraft through the bubbling cauldron.

On returning to Tangmere it was discovered that both aircraft in White Section were missing. Long after the time their fuel would have run out, and checks made at other airfields had failed to locate them, the squadron accepted that two of their pilots would be absent from the mess that evening. It was later confirmed that it was Blair's aircraft which had been seen to blow-up and Marcinkus had probably ditched in the Channel. The photographs now produced here indicate that the Lithuanian did in fact make the French coast, it is possible that he became disorientated during the fight and, after completing his attack, became separated from his colleagues and in the ensuing confusion flew a reciprocal bearing. His damaged Hurricane was recovered by the Germans and broken down for scrap in France.

Marcinkus was captured and eventually sent to Stalag Luft III where he took part in the Great Escape, and was one of those who was shot in cold blood by the Gestapo after recapture. Another pilot who by the end of the day was to become an involuntary guest of the Germans, was Pilot Officer McLeod of 234 Squadron. Flying Spitfire V *AA722*, McLeod took part in an uneventful patrol in the morning and at 12.38 hours was ordered to West Malling where he was to operate with 118 and 501 Squadrons in providing fighter escort for bombers detailed to attack the German flotilla. McLeod and his squadron took-off at 14.15 hours and were soon in action against Bf 109s which were providing an outer protective screen. Flight Lieutenant

MacKay flying Spitfire *BL241* managed to get an enemy aircraft in his sights and fired a short burst at it. The German pilot, surprised by the strikes on his aircraft, made a violent turn to port, collided with a colleague and sent both 109s spinning into the overcast, not to be seen again. Meanwhile, the British fighters became separated in the melee

---

Below and overleaf *Pilot Officer McLeod's Spitfire V AA722 has its 234 Squadron markings AZ and code B coloured Sky, which matches the spinner and fuselage band. The serial is painted aft of the Sky fuselage band just above the tailplane. The middle aircraft is UZ-A of 306 Squadron and carries light grey codes, the serial of this machine is not visible. The third Spitfire is the one flown by Wing Commander Stanford Tuck whose kill markings can be seen on the starboard cowling. The codes of this machine are RS-T and appear to be in Sky. Tuck was not shot down in this machine during the Channel Dash, having already been in captivity for 15 days by the time of 'Operation Fuller'. On January 28 1942, Tuck left Biggin Hill with a Canadian pilot, Flying Officer Harley, as his wing-man. Attacking targets of opportunity as they skimmed across the French countryside at low level, the two Spitfires were caught in cross-fire of the defences around Boulogne. Tuck's machine was hit several times and the ace, with 29 confirmed victories to his credit, crash-landed to captivity.* **Overleaf** *Tuck's Spitfire where it came to rest, the shattered wooden propeller and 29 kill markings being clearly visible.*

and returned individually to West Malling. Pilot Officer Pike in *AA727* and Pilot Officer McLeod in *AA722* were not seen again and failed to return to base. McLeod made it to France and his aircraft ended on the same scrap dump as Marcinkus' Hurricane. These were just two of the 71 aircraft lost by the British in the action. The cost to the Germans was, one patrol boat and 17 aircraft. The three German war ships reached the safety of a new anchorage in Norway on February 13.

A bad day for 41 Squadron

April 12 1942 dawned bright and sunny, ideal weather for the Spitfires of 41 Squadron to carry the war to Germany by escorting bombers on strikes against enemy installations on the continent. The morning passed quietly with 'A' Flight at readiness and 'B' Flight carrying out exercises in formation flying.

At 12.30 hours the squadron was called to readiness and at 12.45 nine aircraft took-off from Merston to join forces with the Tangmere and Northolt wings in escorting 12 Bostons which had been briefed to attack Hazebrouck. Led by their CO, Wing Commander P.H. Hugo, flying *BL248* as one of the aircraft of Red Section, the other two being Flight Sergeant E.G. Watts in *W3450* and Pilot Officer Van Rood in *W3654*, the nine Spitfires met up with their charges and headed towards France.

Soon after crossing the coast the escorts were 'bounced' by enemy fighters and the sky became alive with twisting aircraft. It was every man for himself and on this occasion 41 Squadron came off badly. Flight Lieutenant Van Der Stok flying *BL595* was hit and bailed out over St Omer, and soon after Flight Sergeant Watts' aircraft was seen to be in trouble. As quickly as it started, the dog-fight came to an end, and the mauled Spitfires of 41 Squadron headed back to Merston to count the cost.

Only four of the squadron's nine aircraft returned. Pilot Officer Cambridge *(AD477)* crash landed at Manston, but of Flight Lieutenant Palmer, Flight Lieutenant Van Der Stok, Pilot Officer Van Rood and Flight Sergeant Watts there was no trace. Among the pilots who landed safely back at Merston was Squadron Leader C.J. Fee *(BL514)*, who took over command of the squadron from Wing Commander Hugo later the same day. With five aircraft lost and no claims recorded for the destruction of enemy aircraft, it was certainly a black day for the Squadron Leader's first in command, but better times were around the corner and No 41 went on to more than avenge their comrades who fell in action on April 12.

This page *The wreckage of Flight Sergeant E.G. Watts' Spitfire* W3450, EB-H. *The codes are Sky, as is the fuselage band. The fuselage roundel is a type A1, but no markings can be seen on the undersides of the crumpled wing. The position of the serial on the Sky band is of interest. Unfortunately the Flight Sergeant did not survive the crash.*

'Circus' to Ostend

The day before war was declared 226 Squadron took its Fairey Battles to France as part of 72 Wing of the Advanced Air Striking Force. The campaign in France saw the squadron fighting hard to delay the German advance, but it was all to no avail and they were withdrawn to England in June 1940. From the hostile skies of France the unit moved to Northern Ireland, where it spent several months patrolling the Irish coast. In May 1941 it moved to Wattisham where it converted to Blenheims and began to mount strikes against shipping and land targets in North-West Europe. Stood down from operations in October 1941 the squadron converted to Boston IIIs and was ready to recommence operations in early 1942 from its new base at Swanton Morley.

By this time the RAF was carrying the fight to the Germans with day and night strikes at tactical targets. Daylight 'Circus' operations formed a large part of the Boston's activity and 226 Squadron was to the fore.

As well as attacking troop concentrations, lines of communication and supply dumps, the RAF also concentrated on installations such as power stations in an attempt to create as much disruption as possible as well as to bring the Luftwaffe into the air to fight.

On April 27 1942 226 Squadron was briefed to attack a power station at Ostend and at 13.34 hours, led by Wing Commander Surplice flying *Z2281 'B'*, the following aircraft lifted from the grass of Swanton Morley and headed out over the North Sea: Flight Lieutenant Yates Earl *AL700 'T'*, Pilot Officer Barker *AL278 'W'*, Warrant Officer Corrigan *AL677 'P'*, Sergeant Lyle *Z2295 'A'* and a Canadian, Warrant Officer Keech *Z2249 'D'*. The six Bostons stayed low to avoid the enemy radar then, just before crossing the enemy coast, pulled up to 2,000 feet for their run-in to the target.

Background photograph *Boston III Z2249, MQ-D after it came to rest near Dunkirk. The fuselage roundel is a type A1 and the fin flash has three 8-inch stripes red/white/blue 27 inches high. There are no underwing markings. The camouflage is dark green/earth on top surfaces and Sky on undersurfaces.*

Inset *Individual aircraft letter D appears to be in dark grey but the colours of the Donald Duck motif are not known, the original print shows the figure to be carrying a bomb in the hand raised above the head.*

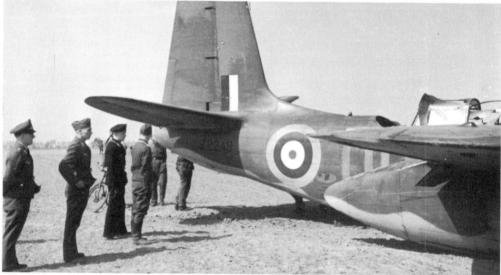

The ground defences threw up a seemingly impenetrable barrage but the six aircraft pushed on and deposited 16 500 lb bombs into the target area. During the approach to the target, Warrant Officer Keech's aircraft was seen to be hit, but he carried on and dropped his bombs on the target before turning his aircraft towards the sea. The others saw the crippled Boston still under control, but with the starboard engine stopped, heading away from the target, then they lost it as they fought their way out.

The five survivors landed back at base at 15.15 hours and after refuelling took off with another aircraft to carry out a sea search for their missing colleague. This proved to be fruitless and the missing aircraft and crew were presumed lost.

After leaving the target, Warrant Officer Keech and his crew, Sergeant Phillips and Sergeant Handford, struggled to keep the ailing Boston in the air. But with one engine out and damage to the starboard wing, this proved to be impossible and eventually the Canadian had to admit defeat and crash-landed the aircraft on open ground near Dunkirk. He and his crew were captured before they could destroy the aircraft which fell almost intact into enemy hands.

The squadron's Operational Record Book which records the incident through the eyes of the other crews, reports that Z2249 lost part of its starboard wing during the attack, close examination of the photographs reveals this not to be so. Just a small example of how mistakes can be made and recorded for posterity during the heat of battle.

It is interesting to record that on June 29 1942 a Boston (AL743 'L') of 226 Squadron was flown by a four-man American crew, Captain Kegleman, Lieutenant Bell, Top Sergeant Golay and Sergeant Cunningham, in a raid against marshalling yards at Hazebrouck. The crew thus becoming the first USAAC personnel to drop bombs on enemy-held territory.

Opposite page top Warrant Officer Keech spends his first moments in captivity enjoying a cigarette, whose size and shape indicates that it probably came from the same packet as the one in the fingers of the Feldwebel to the left of the picture. All German personnel are of das Heer apart from the Luftwaffe Hauptmann on the extreme right of the group. The Hauptmann in the centre of the group is wearing an old pattern service dress cap and appears to have a 1914 EK I on his left pocket. The Oberleutnant next to him has the ribbon of a Kriegsverdienstkreuz II Klasse on his tunic. The group of three looking over his shoulder are all wearing 1938 pattern Feldmütze, and the rifle barrel which can be seen behind the Warrant Officer belongs to a Kar 98k. The ultimate fate of Warrant Officer Keech is not known and attempts to locate him in Canada met with no success.

Centre The starboard wing-tip, which witnesses say was shot away, can be clearly seen still intact, although the same cannot be said for the canopy.

Bottom The inboard flap is in the landing position and oil streaks on the top wing and engine cowling are evidence of the damage suffered. The squadron code letters MQ are in dark grey and serial is black.

Captured for Christmas

The forthcoming Christmas festivities, bringing with them a short respite from operations, were very much in the minds of air and ground crews at Lympne on December 22 1943. But there were still three days to go, three days in which the Typhoons of 1 Squadron could continue taking the war across the Channel, disrupting rail traffic, communications, troops movements and the mysterious so-called 'ski' sites. The latter were high on the list of target priorities, and it was such a site at St Pol-Hesdin that eight Typhoons forming Red and Blue Sections were briefed to attack.

Taking off at 09.05 hours the eight aircraft crossed the Channel at low level to avoid detection by enemy radar, then climbed before diving on to their target and hitting it with their cannon; another successful 'rodeo' which helped to delay the onslaught of the V-1 Flying Bomb, for the 'ski' sites were in fact launching ramps for the German missiles.

Six aircraft returned safely to Lympne but of JP961 'U' flown by Australian, Warrant Officer F.J. Wyatt (Blue 4), and JP237 flown by a Scot, Pilot Officer J.W. Sutherland (Red 4), there was no trace. Enquiries revealed that Wyatt had called for a homing after last being

seen near Edineaux, but since then nothing further had been heard. Wyatt had in fact encountered engine trouble, a not unfamiliar problem with the Sabre engine, and had been forced to crash-land his Typhoon. But of Sutherland there was no trace. The two men were very popular members of the squadron and the ORB records that '. . . their loss will be keenly felt'.

Above *The dark green/ocean grey top surface camouflage, and medium sea grey undersurfaces of JP961 are relatively unmarked as it sits rather forlornly awaiting its fate on a French railway wagon. Fuselage bands and codes are in Sky and the serial/stencil markings in black. The roundel is a type C1 and the fin flash is 24 inches high with 11-inch red/blue stripes either side of a 2-inch white stripe.*

'Ramrod 387'

The code name 'Ramrod' was used to define a straightforward escort operation, where the main objective was for the bombers to destroy their assigned target rather than using them as bait to attract Luftwaffe fighters into combat with RAF fighters.

On December 22 1943 129 (Mysore) Squadron together with 66 Squadron were detailed to provide escort for Mosquitoes attacking construction works in Northern France. Taking off from Hornchurch at 15.15 hours the two squadrons, forming 129 Wing, led by Squadron Leader C. Haw—a holder of the Order of Lenin—accompanied the Mosquitoes at low level before climbing to cross the French Coast west of Dieppe. During the climb scattered cloud was encountered and contact was lost with the bombers, the cloud gradually became thicker

deteriorating from $\frac{6}{10}$ cumulus at 6,000 feet to
total coverage over the target. The Spitfires
circled and occasionally caught glimpses of
the Mosquitoes operating at a lower level,
their presence being indicated by an intense
flak barrage. Turning to make their exit the
escorts also encountered heavy anti-aircraft
fire, one burst causing the Spitfire of Blue 1,
Flying Officer Bradshaw, to collide with Red
4, Flying Officer Cain. Bradshaw in *MH425*
'T', and Cain in *MH441* 'X', evacuated their
stricken aircraft, one landing at St Saens and
the other on the other side of the river.

Squadron Leader Haw in *MH487* 'H',
patrolled the area at between 5,000 and 9,000
feet before diving to low level and leaving the
French coast near Cayeux, arriving back at
Hornchurch at 16.40 hours. The result of the
bombing was inconclusive and the two
Spitfires lost gave a score of 2:0 in favour of
the Germans.

This page *The Spitfire, Mk IX LF of Flying
Officer Bradshaw, being consigned to a German
scrap dump after its recovery. The Merlin 66
shows signs of having been partially buried. The
roundel is a type C1, and codes are in light grey,
the serial, MH425 has been partly overpainted
by the DV codes of 129 Squadron. The 1
Squadron Typhoon seen in the background was
also lost on December 22 and is featured in the
previous story.*

Background photograph *A good air-to-air shot taken from a Ju 88 showing the newly re-painted and repaired Stirling airborne from Gilze Rijen.*

Inset *A Klemm 35D trainer is dwarfed by the Stirling whose damaged nose has not yet been covered by the canvas repair.*

A prize for the Luftwaffe

At 01.25 hours on the morning of 16 August 1942, Sergeant S.C. Orrel opened the throttles of his 7 Squadron Stirling, released the brakes, and set off on his take-off run from Oakington in Cambridgeshire. As the aircraft, serial *N3705* coded *MG-F*, crossed the Norfolk coast and headed for German coastal waters where it was to lay mines, Sergeant T.R. Gough in the rear turret reported that the English coast now lay behind. The dwindling view of the coastline was to be the crew's last look at their homeland for three years, as some five hours later all seven men were to become guests of the German Government, exchanging the comfort of the Oakington Sergeants' Mess for Stalag Luft VIIIB. It would appear that the aircraft's engines started to run rough soon after the mine laying had been accomplished and rather than risk a lengthy sea crossing, Orrel decided to land his aircraft in Holland.

At 06.58 hours the crew took up their crash stations and the pilot put the aircraft down close to the castle at Loevestein near the small town of Gorkum. Local-based German soldiers captured the crew and the Luftwaffe was quickly advised that a practically undamaged Stirling was available for their inspection.

Examination showed that the aircraft had suffered only minor damage to its nose and undercarriage, so it was decided to carry out a salvage operation. A team of technicians from the nearby Luftwaffe base at Gilze Rijen was sent to the crash site and, after carrying out temporary repairs, they watched a Luftwaffe pilot fly the aircraft away from its improvised landing ground.

The flight was made on the evening of September 5, and the following morning the aircraft was airborne again, escorted by a Ju 88. Both aircraft climbed to altitude where the Stirling pilot tentatively carried out manoeuvres before allowing the Ju 88 pilot to carry out simulated attacks. It says much for the skill of the German pilot that he was able to co-operate after such a brief period of handling the unfamiliar bomber, and his confidence was underlined by a low-level beat-up of Gilze Rijen before he landed.

The Stirling stayed at Gilze Rijen, often parked under a camouflaged net alongside the Breda-Tilburg road, until the afternoon of September 18 when, escorted by a KG 2 Do 217, it was flown to the Erprobungsstelle at Rechlin. Unfortunately the trail goes cold at Rechlin and so far it has been impossible to determine the ultimate fate of *N3705*.

At the time of its last RAF operational flight, the aircraft was finished in standard Bomber Command dark earth/green camouflage on the top surfaces, and night black beneath. Codes and serial were all dull red, the 7 Squadron codes *MG* being slightly smaller than the aircraft's individual letter. In Luftwaffe hands, the roundels and codes were overpainted dunkelgrün (71) and crosses painted over them. The under surfaces and two thirds of the fuselage sides were painted yellow (04).

Repairs to the aircraft's nose were carried out by covering the damaged area with canvas then stuffing it with straw. It is interesting to reflect how this may have affected its handling characteristics. The Stirling's crew was: pilot, Sergeant S.C. Orrel; navigator, Sergeant A. Buckley; engineer, Sergeant F. Thompson; wireless operator, Sergeant C.A. Bowers; front gunner, Sergeant J.A. Bond; mid-upper gunner, Sergeant R.A. Holman; rear gunner, Sergeant T.R. Gough.

Above left *Scaffolding enables the lofty nose of the Stirling to be reached with ease. Straw is being stuffed into a canvas covering over the damaged nose area. It is interesting to see that the two Brownings have not been removed. The aircraft in the background is one of KG 2s Do 217s.*

Left *Tape was used to hold the stuffed canvas in place and can be seen being prepared for application.*

Above right *The tape harness is now complete and stretched into place. The undersurfaces have been painted yellow and crosses applied. This view also shows the Stirling's massive flaps.*

Hurricane Odyssey

Together with the Spitfire the Hurricane was immortalised by its major contribution to the Battle of Britain. Hawker's sturdy fighter flew with the RAF throughout the war in every theatre of operations, and as well as being used as an interceptor also gave a good account of itself as a fighter bomber, night intruder, ground attack aircraft and night fighter. The following collection of photographs tell their own story.

Right *A Mk I Hurricane abandoned in France during the May 1940 withdrawal.*

Left *Abandoned in France. This Hurricane suffers the ignominy of being pushed into a ditch as new 'tenants' occupy its airfield. Souvenir hunters have stripped it of all identification. The triangle in front of the fin is a 'gas panel'.*

Below left *This Hurricane, believed to have been operated by 501 Squadron in France, shares its last resting place with a 12 Squadron Fairey Battle. Damage to the fuselage makes positive identification of the serial difficult. It looks like P2859 but this Hurricane was used by various squadrons and OTUs until it became an instructional airframe in 1944. It is more likely to be P5959 which was a Gloster Aircraft-built Mk I.*

Top right and right *Hurricanes with an odd mottled camouflage on their wing leading edges were operated by 3 Squadron RAAF in the Balkans, it is possible that these two were used by that unit. The high gloss spinner on one of the aircraft is of interest.*

Below right *Believed to have been a 213 Squadron aircraft, this Hurricane was found in the desert by an Afrika Korps patrol. The pilot had not been injured in the landing but had died from exposure and thirst, his body being found under the port wing. The patrol gave him a Christian burial then destroyed the aircraft, which it is interesting to see still had a black painted underside to its port wing. It is not known how long it had been in the desert but the date it was discovered was February 22 1942.*

Heinz Joachim Marseilles was one of Germany's most famous
aces and became a legend in the desert where he flew with JG 27.
This 213 Squadron Hurricane was shot down in February 1942
and is seen being examined by Marseilles, who became known as
'The Star of Africa'. This Hurricane was one of his 158 victims,
probably being among the first 48 which earned him the award of
a Knight's Cross on February 24 1942. He was killed on
September 30 1942, after bailing out of his famous Bf 109F-4
(Trop) Yellow 14, and striking the tailplane.

Above left and left *The name* Kiwi *suggests a New Zealand pilot for this Hurricane I, serial Z4932. The unit is not certain but 185 Squadron operating from Hal Far is known to have used the codes GL which fit those mutilated on the aircraft. The aircraft's windscreen shows evidence of battle damage.*

Below left *The single letter identity* X *was used by 229 Squadron when it was operating from Malta, so this could well be one of the unit's Mk IIas. The serial is repeated above the fin flash and the name* Laura *is in script beneath the cockpit.*

Above and below *Hurricanes wrecked in North Africa, the armament has been removed from both of them.*

The Battle's last battle

The Fairey Battle was another type chosen for full-scale production during the RAF's Expansion Programme of the late 1930s. By the time the war started in 1939 it was outdated and proved no match for the modern Luftwaffe fighters. Nonetheless it equipped units of the Advanced Air Striking Force which flew to France on September 2 1939 and contributed to the attempts made to stem the enemy advance. Perhaps the most notable exploit involving the Battle was the attack by 12 Squadron, on May 12 1940, on the bridge at Veldwezelt over the Albert Canal, which resulted in the award of the Victoria Cross to Flying Officer E. Garland and his observer, Sergeant T. Gray.

Below *This 12 Squadron Battle PH-Y, N2150, is similar to that flown by Flying Officer Garland on May 12 1940. This particular aircraft was taken on charge by the unit on May 23 1940 and was reported as being burned at Nantes with other abandoned aircraft. If this is*

so, then the destruction must have been carried out by the Germans after this photograph was taken! On some Battles the serial was painted on the fuselage and rudder, but this one seems only to have the latter.

Right and below right *Battle JN-C was L5540 of 150 Squadron. It was taken on charge on May 3 1940 and lost on May 10 during a raid on the Meuse bridges. The fin stripes are painted down the rudder hinge line, and the serial appears only on the rear fuselage.*

Bottom right *This collection of scrapped aircraft is worthy of considerable study. The Battles in the foreground are both ex-88 Squadron aircraft. L5462 was taken on charge on May 19 1940 and lost in action seven days later. The individual letter seems to have been changed from E to G during the aircraft's one week with the unit. VO-T is K9202 which was issued to 98 Squadron on May 16 1940, it is interesting as many people have claimed that 98 Squadron never used the VO code on their Battles. Other aircraft, which can be seen on the original print, are Hurricanes. To the left can be seen a set of Battle mainplanes still in their crate.*

Battered Blenheims

The Blenheim was ordered into production 'straight off the drawing board' as part of the RAF's Expansion Programme in 1935. At the time of the Munich Crisis 16 Bomber Command squadrons were equipped with the short-nosed Blenheim 1, and the aircraft entered overseas service with 30 Squadron at Habbanyia in January 1938. Within an hour of the declaration of war, a Blenheim Mk 1V *(N6215)* of 139 Squadron, piloted by Flying Officer A. McPherson, left its base at Wyton to carry out a reconnaissance of the German naval installation at Wilhelmshaven, thus becoming the first RAF aircraft to enter enemy airspace. Although outclassed the Blenheim carried out sterling work as a bomber, fighter and strike aircraft, and as well as operating from bases in England, was also used in India, Egypt, Greece and the Middle East. It was used extensively to carry the war to the continent during 1941-2, and from Malta it performed legion service in attacking enemy shipping.

This page *This Blenheim Mk IV (L9191) believed to be code* E *or* L *of 18 Squadron, was taken on charge by the unit on February 13 1940, and destroyed on May 19 1940 during the retreat from France. The location is probably Crecy, from which the squadron operated before returning to Lympne.*

Top *A poignant symbol of the debacle of France 1940.*
Above and below *A Mk IV of an unknown unit showing signs of considerable damage. Modellers who like making dioramas would do well to study the exit marks of the bullets around the A type roundel.*

This page and right *A trio of photographs of a 114 Squadron Mk IV Blenheim abandoned at Condé Vraux, France, in 1940. What appears to be a black cross under the port wing are, in fact, open access panels. The dorsal turret housing a single machine-gun has been modified from that fitted as standard. The roundel is a type A and the full codes are WT-L, no fin flash is carried.*

Right *A Mk I Blenheim of 113 Squadron probably photographed in Greece during 1940. Codes are VA-W, and it is interesting to note how the A has been partly painted on the large wing root fillet.*

Below right *The code YH was used by both 21 and 11 Squadrons. 11 operated its Blenheims in the Middle East and it is believed that YH-L, a Mk IV, was photographed in Crete. The individual letter L is painted over the yellow ring of the type A1 roundel.*

Above *A completely devastated Mk I Blenheim destroyed by its original owners to prevent it falling intact into the hands of the enemy. The underwing type A roundel is remarkably undamaged.*

Below *Consigned to a lonely end in the desert, this Mk IV gives up some of its secrets to two inquisitive Germans.*

Wimpy parade

Taking its nickname from J. Wellington Wimpy, a character in the *Daily Mirror* 'Popeye' strip cartoon, the Wellington will always have its own niche in RAF history. One of the first bombers to take the air war to the German homeland, the Wellington served throughout the war with great distinction. It was popular with crews and its geodetic construction, designed by Barnes Wallis, enabled it to absorb a tremendous amount of punishment. The following selection of photographs show those aircraft which, for one reason or another, 'failed to return'.

Below *Probably the most reproduced photograph of a Wellington in enemy hands. This particular aircraft (T2501) is a 99 Squadron machine which failed to return from operations on December 4 1940. The aircraft was one of ten which left Newmarket to carry out 3 Group's Order No B325. The crew was, Flying Officer F.H. Vivian, Pilot Officer H.G. de Forest, Pilot Officer J.R. Hoppe, and Sergeants Gage, Bush and Wright. Six aircraft returned to base and three landed at other airfields; Mildenhall, Martlesham Heath and West Raynham. Only T2516, flown by Flight Lieutenant Harvey, found a suitable target in the Ruhr area, the rest abandoned the trip due to bad weather.*

Right *The twin .303 Browning machine-guns in the nose turret of T2501.*

Left *A close-up of the crossed tennis racquets and balls painted just below the cockpit on the port side of* T2501.

Below *German personnel show a lot of interest in the Nash and Thompson rear turret of Wellington Ic* T2501. *The man to the left is an Unteroffizier and to his right is a Gefreiter who is wearing an EK II ribbon on his tunic. The man on the extreme right is wearing a 1936 pattern helmet and his rifle appears to be a G98.*

Above *Wellingtons were used by OCUs and were sometimes flown on 'easy' trips by trainee crews and an instructor to give the feeling of operational conditions. The OCUs provided such crews for the famous 1,000-bomber raids early in the war. This particular Wellington comes from either 25 or 26 OTU, its mutilated codes preventing positive identification. 25 used codes PP and 26 PB, both of which would fit. The roundel is a type C1 which came into general use in May 1942.*

Right *The interior of the OCU Wellington clearly showing the geodetic construction.*

Left *A Luftwaffe Leutnant examines the rear Frazer Nash turret and its twin .303 Brownings, of the Wellington featured in the previous two photographs.*

Right *The fin/rudder of the Wellington has been broken off, hence giving the appearance of the nose turret, but examination clearly shows part of the tailplane fairing on the left-hand side of the fuselage. The Leutnant has collar patches in 'Goldgelb' and his cuff band reads 'Kriegsberichter der Luftwaffe', he also wears the ribbon of an EK II and the Bardfunkerabz on his right breast pocket.*

Right *Having examined the outside of the turret the Leutnant now tries the gunner's seat for size.*

Left *All identification has been stripped from this Wellington which came to grief in the Middle East and is being subjected to very close examination.*

Below left *A film cameraman records another success for the Luftwaffe, and no doubt this formed the story-line of a subsequent news film. The collector ring and cowling, which is open on the inboard side, as well as the exhaust and fuel octane rating on the wing leading edge, are features rarely seen quite as clearly as this on contemporary British prints.*

Above right *In addition to the under-carriage detail this photograph also provides useful information about the style of lace-up boots worn by German personnel in the desert.*

Right *'Number, rank and name' are probably the only answers being given by the Flight Sergeant air gunner.*

Inset *Another air gunner looks to be on the point of sharing a joke with the cameraman . . . but then perhaps he had seen the arrival of sustenance* (**background photograph**). *The 'sparks' badge on his tunic indicates that he was also the wireless operator.*

Above *The Sergeant Pilot of the Wellington posed in front of one of Mussolini's edifices to the 'New Empire' which was quickly christened 'Marble Arch' by the British Tommies.*

Below *Off to captivity. All propaganda photographs having been taken, the six RAF crewmen share the back of an open car. One chooses to wear his Irvin jacket but the others have thrown theirs in the back. The men are wearing 1940 style tunics and side hats, although the co-pilot sitting on the right-hand side seems to have acquired a most unconventional hat.*

Stirling scrap

This page *The remains of a 149 Squadron Stirling, identified by the codes OJ, litter the German countryside, a very typical scene the morning after a Bomber Command night raid. Nothing is known about this particular aircraft or its loss. The rear turret has been completely broken off and conveniently shows the rather primitive Elsan toilet installed for the crew's use. No doubt a very uncomfortable place to be caught with one's trousers down.*

A process of elimination

The easiest method of identifying any specific aircraft is by its serial, in most cases this proves foolproof and the aircraft's record card leads the researcher to its date of acceptance, service use and the date it was finally struck off charge. In some cases mistakes are made, especially by crew members writing serials in their log books, or the unit diarist making an incorrect entry. It is also not unknown for a machine to be painted with an incorrect serial or to use spare parts from a different aircraft carrying a different serial; an example of the latter will come to light in the story of a B-24. But what can be done to identify an aircraft whose serial is not known? The answer is, quite a lot if other facts are available. The photograph of a 15 Squadron Stirling 'U' for Uncle was too good not to include and with the help of Michael J.F. Bowyer its almost certain identity was discovered.

Close examination of the photograph quickly reveals that the aircraft cannot be a Mk III because they were not fitted with the FN7 dorsal turret. The window layout confirms that it is in fact a Mk I, so any Stirling later than 1942 carrying *LS-U* can be discounted. The A1 fuselage roundel makes it

a pre-change to type C, and as the change in 3 Group was quite rapid we can assume the picture to be around the pre-mid July 1942 period.

Code letters seem to be a very light grey used by some 15 and 7 Squadron aircraft, the change to red letters came in May and again

The crumpled underneath of the fuselage indicates that Pilot Officer Patterson carried out a belly landing after encountering trouble over Germany. The light grey codes and A1 roundel are clearly visible, and the aircraft does seem to be in remarkably good condition. Nothing is known of its eventual fate. Codes OF on the fuselage of the aircraft behind the nose were used by 97 Squadron who were operating Lancasters in August 1942 when this photograph is believed to have been taken. Close examination of the original print does, however, indicate that the fuselage with OF codes has the top camouflage segregated from the black by a wavy line which was used on the unit's Manchesters.

The four .303 Browning machine-guns which provided the sting in the Stirling's tail, and their Frazer Nash turret, being examined by a German engineer after the capture of R9153.

was implemented fairly quickly, so we are looking for a likely pre-May machine.

The window arrangement aft indicates a fairly early Stirling although this is not entirely foolproof as many ad hoc modifications were made and it would be quite impossible to say which windows were where and when. The FN7 turret came into use in mid-1941 but few aircraft were equipped with it by August, *N3662*, etc, and *N6066* from Belfast were supplied with the turret but later on some earlier examples were modified to accept it. Stirlings carrying the codes *LS-U* were, *N6045*, *N3676*, *R9304*, *R9153* and *R9201*. Of these *N3676* had an FN7 turret but went from 15 Squadron to 1652 OCU on April 8 1942, similarly *R9304* also joined the same OCU shortly after. *R9201* was lost on a mining trip to the Gironde estuary on July 6/7 1942, and *N6045* did not have a dorsal turret; this aircraft being lost during a raid on Brest on September 7 1941.

This leaves *R9153* which joined 15 Squadron on July 31 1942 and failed to return from Nuremburg on the night of August 28/29 1942. This aircraft was completed in June and the dates are acceptable, although it is a little odd that it was still carrying outdated markings at the end of August.

However, none of the other '*U*' Uncles, which include *W7518*, originally '*C*' then '*U*', then '*G*' and finally '*W*', which was shot down by a night fighter over Holland on March 1/2 1943, fit the bill so we are back to *R9153*. This aircraft appears to have taken over the '*U*' code from *W7518* on or about July 28 1942 and carried out its first trip to Osnabruck on August 9 1942 in the hands of Sergeant Russell-Collins when it was damaged by flak. Repairs were completed two days later when it was taken on a raid to Mainz by the same pilot. It was one of the Stirlings which moved to Bourn on August 13 1942 and carried out its first trip from that airfield on August 15 when once again Sergeant Russell-Collins was in command. The same crew visited Frankfurt on August 24 then four days later Pilot Officer Patterson and his crew flew it on what turned out to be its last trip in the hands of 15 Squadron to Nuremburg.

Loaded with incendiaries '*U*' left Bourn at 20.35 hours with seven other aircraft, one of which soon aborted with a mechanical malfunction. The others pressed on to the target which was clear of cloud and could be seen from several miles away. Of the seven aircraft which made the trip, '*U*' failed to return, one landed at Manston, another at Tangmere and yet another at Oakington. There seems to be little doubt that the aircraft in the accompanying photographs is *R9153*, and its grey codes only serve to indicate that not all instructions as to the changes of camouflage and markings were carried out at the time the instruction was issued; a belief often held by many 'experts'. The crew of '*U*' on its last trip was: Pilot Officer Patterson, Sergeant Oswin, Flight Sergeant Gilson, Flight Sergeant Lawrence, Sergeant Payne, Sergeant Hawthorne and Sergeant Ludgate.

Carrying the standard day fighter scheme of ocean grey and dark green top surfaces and medium grey undersurfaces. Codes and fuselage band are Sky and the roundel is a type C1. The badge below the windscreen cannot be identified. Propeller blades have broken off in the crash and the partially lowered flaps can be seen under the port wing. The small black dot at the 2 o'clock position on the roundel is the location point for part of the IFF (Identification Friend or Foe) aerial which stretches from this point on both fuselage sides to the tips of the tailplanes.

Foray to France

In August 1942 340 (Ile de France) Squadron moved from Hornchurch to Biggin Hill where it started to re-equip with Spitfire Mk IXs. The squadron was the first Free French fighter squadron to form in England, or to be more correct, at Turnhouse in Scotland, which it did in November 1941 with Spitfire Mk IIs. After a period of working-up it moved to the west coast of Scotland in January 1942 before moving to become part of the Tangmere wing in April. The following months saw the unit very active in 'Ramrod' and 'Circus' operations and also playing its part in the Dieppe raid.

The move to Kent saw operations continuing in the same vein but the arrival of the more powerful Mk IXs enabled the unit to meet the increasing threat of the FW 190 with greater confidence. The last day of October 1942 brought dull overcast weather with $\frac{9}{10}$ cloud at 1,200 feet and a north wind, not ideal conditions for fighter sweeps. But the AOC had other ideas and the unit was detailed to mount a four aircraft strike against railway targets in the Dunkerque-Calais area.

Lieutenant Fournier flying 'O' BS533, and Sous Lieutenant Demas in 'Y' BS394, formed Blue Section and Red Section comprised Capitaine Chauvin and Lieutenant Helies in 'L' BS243, and 'B' BS535, respectively.

The four Spitfires, led by Lieutenant Fournier, who was to take command of the squadron the following April, took off from Biggin Hill and were soon lost in the low cloud. The target area was covered by $\frac{9}{10}$ cloud down to 1,500 feet, but the aircraft descended through a convenient gap and sought their targets.

Blue Section was attracted to a goods train heading for Dunkerque and headed at low level line abreast to give it their undivided attention. Ten miles south-east of the target they successfully skirted heavy ground fire before carrying out considerable modifications to the train with their guns, then climbed to the sanctuary of the scudding overcast. Meanwhile Red Section headed for St Omer seeking similar targets. After advising the leader of their intentions nothing further was heard from either aircraft, and Blue Section returned alone.

Lieutenant Fournier encountered hydraulic troubles on reaching Biggin and crashed on landing following a flapless approach and total brake failure. The other Blue Section Spitfire was undamaged, so on this occasion the cost of damage to one enemy freight train, was one severely damaged aircraft and two complete losses. A seemingly unsatisfactory balance, but no one knows what the train was carrying, or how vital its supplies were; such are the fortunes of war.

'Circus 119'

The code name 'Circus' was given to a day-light attack by heavily escorted light bombers mounted against targets within the escort fighters' range, with the prime objective of bringing enemy fighters into action, thereby forcing the Luftwaffe into maintaining a strong defensive force in the areas concerned. The operation against St Omer station on April 4 1942 achieved the objective, although it cost 303 Squadron both its Ops Room Controller and 'B' Flight Commander.

303 Squadron formed at Northolt on August 2 1940 under the command of Squadron Leader R.G. Kellet, and although it was the second Polish fighter squadron to form in the RAF, it became the first to see action with 11 Group during the Battle of Britain.

On April 4 1942, still at Northolt, but now under the command of Squadron Leader Kolaczkowski, the unit was ordered to join forces with 316 and 317 Squadrons, to form the escort for 12 Bostons detailed to attack St Omer.

Using the call sign 'Boiler', 12 Spitfires took off from Northolt at 9.40 hours and rendezvoused east of Chatham at 10.03 hours before heading for France where they patrolled the coast at 21,000 feet. Light flak was seen over Boulogne and the fighters soon detected their charges flying at 17,000 feet and turned north of Hardelot to cover them over the target.

The Bostons separated into two boxes of six, one section turning sharply to port and descending while the second made a shallower turn and held their height for a few minutes longer. A glint of sun on metal warned 303 that other aircraft were above them and they turned to face two sections of Bf 109Fs and FW 190s, placing themselves between the enemy fighters and the diving Bostons. Meanwhile eight more FW 190s were seen approaching from the direction of Boulogne and 316 turned to meet the new threat which by now had formed into four sections of two and attacked the Spitfires in line astern.

Flying Officer Horbalzewski of 'A' Flight in *AD940* tussled with an FW 190 and sent it spinning down out of control then left the fight to escort a damaged Boston to the Kent coast, Flight Sergeant Popek, his 'A' Flight colleague in *AD116* having already accounted for the FW 190 which had attacked the bomber.

Two 303 Squadron pilots were heard to make distress calls, but in the melee their individual call sign numbers were not heard, although one was reported to be landing his damaged aircraft in France. On return to Northolt, Flight Lieutenant Daszewski 'B' Flight Commander (Boiler 15) in *AD455* and Flight Lieutenant Kustrzynski (Boiler 51) in *AB824*, were missing. So names could be put against the two men who had made the radio transmissions during the combat. Flight Lieutenant Kustrzynski was the Ops Room Controller and he was the pilot who landed his damaged Spitfire in France where it was recovered by the Luftwaffe.

Left *The Castle Bromwich-built Spitfire Vb of Flight Lieutenant Kustrzynski being hoisted aboard a recovery truck for transportation to a scrap dump. The aircraft is finished in standard RAF day fighter camouflage of the period and carries a type A1 roundel between its Sky coloured codes.*

Above *With the fuselage safely aboard the truck, attention is given to getting the starboard wing alongside it. The badge below the windscreen is the famous emblem of 111 'Kosciuszko' Squadron Polish Air Force. It is very likely that the aircraft also carried the red/white chequered Polish national insignia just behind the spinner below the exhaust stacks.*

Below *All stowed and ready to go. Note how dark the undersurfaces appear and how they are devoid of all markings. The pointed posts are the tripods of the lifting equipment.*

A watery grave

485 Squadron was the first New Zealand fighter squadron to form in the UK, this taking place at Driffield on March 1 1941. In 1942 it was heavily engaged on 'Circus' and 'Ramrod' operations and towards the autumn of the year its Vb aircraft suffered heavily at the hands of the FW 190.

On March 26 1942 it formed part of the escort for Bostons attacking Le Havre and on leaving the target area was bounced by several enemy aircraft. Caught unawares and with fuel running low, the squadron tried to escape and put up a good fight with Flight Lieutenant Compton in *W3747* gaining a Bf 109 which dived straight into the sea after a four-second burst from his Spitfire's guns. But Flight Sergeant Krebs, flying the regular mount of Pilot Officer Clouston, *W3577*, was not so lucky. His aircraft was hit several times and he was forced to land it on the beach.

It is interesting to note that although this loss is recorded in the unit's Operational Record Book during 'Ramrod 17' on March 26, the aircraft appears on several occasions after this date in the hands of Pilot Officers Griffiths and Falls. A good example of how the unwary can be caught by assuming that what is written in official records must be true!

The Spitfire Vb of Flight Sergeant Krebs at rest in the sea. Codes are OU-O and the aircraft carries the name Southland II *on its cowling, this might well refer to the south island of New Zealand. The legend under the windscreen cannot be read even under very great enlargement, but might well be 'Pilot Officer Clouston' who seems to have been the regular pilot before Flight Sergeant Krebs left Kenley in it for its last trip at 15.10 hours on March 26 1942.*

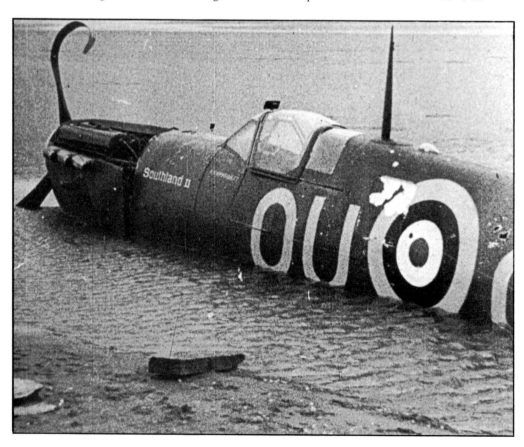

The end of a Halifax

The Halifax has never received the same amount of publicity as the illustrious Lancaster. But it has a record of which it can be justly proud and crews who operated it are invariably ready to defend it most strongly when comparisons are made.

These photographs depict a scene which must have been very common in Germany the morning after Bomber Command's visits. Wreckage marked the route in and out of the target, and in many cases was the metal tomb or funeral pyre of gallant airmen. This particular aircraft was a 102 Squadron machine but no further details are known. 102 is perhaps best known as the unit with which Group Captain Leonard Cheshire was serving, when as a Pilot Officer on the night of February 12/13 1940 flying Whitley Mk V *P5005 'N'*, he received the immediate award of a DSO following his part in an attack on an oil refinery at Wesseling. He was later awarded a Victoria Cross for his four years of operations with Bomber Command. 102 received their first Halifaxes in December 1941 and flew various marks of the aircraft until the end of the war.

Above right *The triangular fin, which still seems to be defiantly pointing skywards, indicates either a B Mk I Series I or II, a B Mk II Series I or perhaps a B Mk V Series I. The top of the fin is to the left in the picture.*

Right *The personnel examining the wreckage are, from left to right, a Flieger, an Unteroffizier, a Leutnant and a Feldwebel. The Leutnant is wearing an EK I, an Observer's badge and a wound badge, it is possible that he is serving with a night fighter unit; maybe the one responsible for the demise of the British bomber?*

Above *The codes* DY *appear to be grey, which was changed from May 1942 onwards, so the date could well be before this period but this is by no means certain. The roundel is a type C1 and the legend beside it reads* DONT FORGET THE DR COMPASS.

Spitfire graveyard

Below EB-W *was a Spitfire of 41 Squadron. It carried the name* Peggy *below the windscreen and had a 25-inch diameter type C1 roundel between the Sky coloured codes. The aircraft in the background is RF-S, AB824, of 303 Squadron, see 'Circus 119' on page 50.*

Lockheed Type 14

This page and overleaf top *Two Lockheed
Type 14s were used in the Middle East and these
photographs reveal the ultimate fate of one of
them. The two machines were Lockheed Nos
1417 and 1496, ex-NC2333 and NC17398,
they were given serials AX681 and 682. This
aircraft is AX682, it is probably finished in
sand/stone camouflage and carries a type A1
roundel. The desert has taken its toll and the
aircraft, from which it is easy to see the lineage
of the Hudson and Ventura, is in a very sorry
state.*

The Desert Hawks

Below *Kittyhawk I HS-A is believed to be AK800 which served with 3 Squadron RAAF before being taken on charge by 260 Squadron RAF on November 12 1941. It crashed near Sidi Barrani on March 5 1942 and was photographed by the Germans on April 6 the same year.*

Left *The Tomahawk is a 40 Squadron SAAF aircraft captured practically intact. The German personnel are perhaps having their first close-up examination of an American-built fighter aircraft.*

Miss Quachita's last date

Miss Quachita was a Douglas-built B-17F *(42-3040)* of the 323 Bomb Squadron, 91 Bomb Group based at Bassingbourn. On the morning of February 21 1944, her Captain, Second Lieutenant Spencer K. Osterberg was briefed to take her and his crew on their fourth Eighth Air Force mission to Gutersloh. The crew, who had started their tour on February 6 with a run to Nancy in France, checked their equipment as they contemplated their third visit to Germany, the other two having been on February 11 and the previous day. Navigator, Second Lieutenant Morris Roy, passed the course to the rendezvous point over King's Lynn and soon the B-17 had formed up with the rest of the squadron and was heading for the Dutch coast with a crossing point north of Amsterdam. The trip was uneventful until the formation reached Hanover, when the glint of sun on metal warned the bomber crews that enemy fighters were above them.

Four FW 190s of II/JG 1 peeled off to attack, their target being the unfortunate *Miss Quachita*. Top Sergeant Lambert Brostrom in the top turret, called 'Fighters at 4 o'clock' and opened fire with his twin Savage-built .50-inch calibre machine-guns.

Osterberg and bombardier, First Lieutenant George Zebrowski, saw one of the FW 190s fall away with smoke pouring from it, then their attention was drawn to more fighters reported by co-pilot, Second Lieutenant Van

John Beran whose R/T call 'More fighters from 2 o'clock' alerted the gunners to further danger. The tail and waist gunners sent a hail of bullets in the direction of the German fighters which by now had raked the B-17 from nose to tail. The top turret guns were silenced and, on going to investigate, a crew member found Brostrom had been killed in the first pass, immediately after his initial warning. The FW 190s continued to press home their attack, killing Lieutenant Beran and wounding the radio-operator, Top Sergeant Harold Klem, and the left waist gunner, Staff Sergeant Clayton Morningstar.

By now the Fortress was crippled, and 15 miles south of Hanover, unable to maintain the altitude of 25,000 feet, it left the formation. At approximately 13.00 hours the two wounded crew members were ordered to bail out since they required urgent medical treatment and they left the aircraft at 23,000 feet.

Any hopes that Lieutenant Osterberg had of reaching England gradually faded and at

Major Heinz Bär (left) and his wing-man, Leo Schuhmacher, wearing the fur-lined leather jacket, examine the shapely nose-art which is typical of that carried by many B-17s and B-24s. Note the damage to the plexiglass nose cone and wing-root.

15.30 hours he belly-landed the aircraft near Lingen about 30 miles from the Dutch border. The surviving crew members attempted to destroy the B-17 but were prevented from doing so by members of the equivalent to the Home Guard led by a man named Berger. The six survivors were taken into custody and moved to Oldenburg before going on to Oberursel and a POW Camp. The two men killed in the combat were buried at Lingen and the two who bailed out received medical treatment before they also were moved to a POW Camp.

The pilot credited with the destruction of *Miss Quachita*, was Major Heinz Bär who, by the end of the war had achieved 220 victories and had been shot down on 18 occasions. He survived the war and died on April 28 1957. Bär's wingman during the fight with the B-17, was Leo Schuhmacher who in 1940 had been a pilot with 2/ZG 76 based in Norway, and flown a Bf 110 in the famous action on December 18 1939 over the Schillig anchorage, when a force of RAF Wellingtons was decimated.

The crew of *Miss Quachita* on February 21 was: pilot, Second Lieutenant Spencer Osterberg; co-pilot, Second Lieutenant Van John Beran; navigator, Second Lieutenant Morris Roy Jr; bombardier, First Lieutenant George Zebrowski; engineer, Top Sergeant Lambert Brostrom; right waist gun, Staff Sergeant Alexander Siatkowski; left waist gun, Staff Sergeant Clayton Morningstar; radio operator, Top Sergeant Harold Klem, ball turret gunner, Staff Sergeant Samuel Aldridge; tail gunner, Staff Sergeant Jay Milewski.

Opposite page top *The B-17 was inspected by a Luftwaffe team led by Leutnant Radetzky who declared it 30 per cent damaged and possible to salvage for further use. Armament and radio equipment were removed and inspected by Dipl Ing Toberg and Sergeant Hoevel, but the fate of the aircraft is not known. Extensive damage to the fin can be clearly seen.*

Centre *Bär, Schuhmacher, and a Feldwebel inspect the turret of Top Sergeant Brostrom. The name below the co-pilot's window may well refer to a girl-friend. It was not an uncommon practice for crews to paint such names by their work stations.*

Bottom *Damage caused by the FW 190s' cannon shells is very evident in this view of* Miss Quachita. *The life raft has inflated automatically during the landing and now rests on the port wing.*

Above *A Feldwebel examines the navigator's station, behind him can be seen one of the Savage-built .50 calibre nose guns of the B-17.*

The oil run

Disruption of fuel supplies played a vital part in the ultimate defeat of Germany. By the end of the war lack of fuel caused serious problems not only to the Luftwaffe but all mechanised arms of the German forces. Oil refineries and storage depots therefore became important targets as far as the strategic bombing campaign was concerned and the Fifteenth Air Force from their bases in Italy made an invaluable contribution against such targets.

On August 29 1944 B-17s of 2 Bomb Group 429 Squadron based at Amendola, Italy, were detailed to take part in a bombing raid against the refinery at Privoser, Czechoslovakia, among them was B-17G *42-97915* flown by Second Lieutenant John Fitzpatrick. This Fortress, which was a Vega (Lockheed) built aircraft, was finished in natural metal overall and carried the black 'Y' in a circle marking of 2 Bomb Group on its fin. Its rudder, elevators and wing tips were painted black and matched the de-icer boots in being the only parts to contrast with the silver airframe.

The squadron rendezvoused at co-ordinates 41-50N/16-10E and headed for their first turning point at 43-25N/16-59E, which took them on practically a direct route to the target. Weather was good as far as the bomber crews were concerned with $\frac{8}{10}$ to $\frac{10}{10}$ cloud from 5 to 20,000 feet giving them good cover. The Luftwaffe appreciated the need to defend their oil supplies as tenaciously as possible, so it came as no surprise to the men of the 429th when hostile fighters were sighted. Colonel Cunningham, the leader of the Group formation, called the B-17s' attention to the fighters, which by now were being engaged by the bombers' escorts. At approximately 11.43 hours, Staff Sergeant E. McClish, the tail gunner of B-17 number *858*, which was flying as the third plane of the first element in the first wave, saw Lieutenant Fitzpatrick's aircraft under attack and reported it turning away with white smoke pouring from the No 3 engine. The Sergeant watched the stricken B-17 turn back in the direction from which it had come and descend into cloud, he noted the position as being 48-55N/18-03E. Some time later McClish's pilot, Lieutenant Charles Crafton heard *915* call for fighter escort, this call also being heard by the co-pilot of another 429 Squadron aircraft, Lieutenant S. Johnson, but neither man heard any reply or further transmissions from the damaged B-17.

Lieutenant Fitzpatrick was unable to maintain height and rather than risk bailing out in the dense cloud, he and his crew stayed with *915* which broke cloud at low level over Hungary. The pilot carried out a perfect crash landing in open country at 46-33N/18-35E and all ten men were taken into captivity. The four officers ending up at Stalag Luft III and the six NCOs at Stalag Luft IV.

The crew on *915*'s last mission was: pilot, Second Lieutenant John Fitzpatrick; co-pilot, Second Lieutenant Charles McGhee; navigator, Second Lieutenant Richard Hausler; bombardier, Second Lieutenant Paul Sumner; engineer, Top Sergeant Eugene Moriarty; left waist gunner, Staff Sergeant Vincent Contrada; right waist gunner, Staff Sergeant John Molitor; radio operator, Staff Sergeant Eugene Black; tail gunner, Staff Sergeant James DeLutes Jr; ball turret gunner, Staff Sergeant Vincente Martinez.

Above *Hungarian soldiers mount guard over the wreck of B-17G 42-97915. The commencement of the black painted areas on the wings can be seen just outboard of the landing light, the rudder is also black.*

Below left *Forced landings in the B-17G often resulted in the chin turret being forced into the fuselage, the apparent lack of damage on this occasion suggests perhaps a combination of soft ground and a very skilful landing. The black wing band markings can be seen on the starboard wing.*

Below *The outer starboard engine was feathered before the crash and has therefore suffered no damage to its blades.*

Above *The waist gunner's position looking forward towards the radio compartment. The guns are Savage-built .50 calibre machine-guns.*

Left *One of the stowage compartments for survival equipment is examined by a Hungarian soldier whose headgear is unique.*

Above right *The flight deck of B-17G 42-97915 from which souvenir hunters, or an evaluation team, have already removed some instruments, those missing being the flight indicator and directional gyro from the top row, and ASI, altimeter, turn and bank indicator, and rate-of-climb indicator from the bottom row. The four instruments in the white square are manifold pressure gauges in the top row and rev counters in the bottom. Flight details are on the card below the throttles in the centre quadrant. The Boeing insignia is carried in the centre-boss of the control columns.*

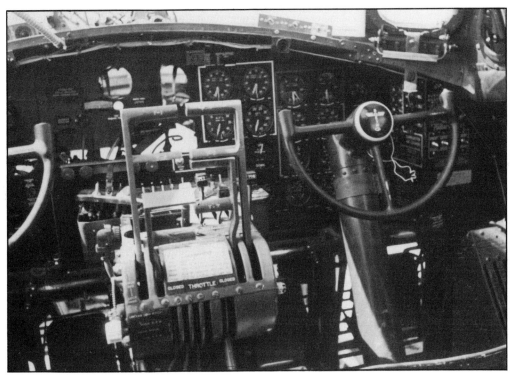

Mission to Oschersleben

Scattered stratocumulus cloud from 2 to 5,000 feet giving between $\frac{4}{10}$ and $\frac{5}{10}$ coverage presented no problems, or indeed gave much cover, to the B-17s of the 533 Bomb Squadron, 381 Bomb Group, as they winged their way over Germany at 27,000 feet on February 22 1944. The Group was heading for Oschersleben, and among them was the Vega-built B-17G *(42-97474)* of First Lieutenant Francis Fridgen and his crew who were on their fourteenth mission. Visibility was over six miles beyond which a haze made sighting of hostile aircraft difficult. But it was good weather for the defending fighters and soon the crews of the Fortresses saw several black dots descending on them from above. The dots materialised into Bf 109s and FW 190s and soon the Eighth Air Force crews were once again running the gauntlet, fighting their way into and out of the target area.

Lieutenant Fridgen's aircraft filled with the smell of cordite as the gunners fired at the enemy fighters and it was quickly in trouble as cannon shells tore away some of its control cables. The navigator, Lieutenant Paul Ehmann and the left waist gunner, Staff

Sergeant Oliver Gaby, were seriously wounded in the first attack and took no further part in the action. As the B-17 slipped from the formation, the fighters pounced again, this time Staff Sergeant William Reilly manning the gun in the radio compartment was wounded in the head, shoulder and leg, reducing the aircraft's defensive capability even further. To add to the crew's problems, fire started inside the fuselage and the order to abandon the aircraft was given.

Top Sergeants Reilly and Brennan, the top turret gunner, together with Staff Sergeant Walter Abernathy, who had manned the right waist gun, bailed out through the bomb-bay and landed safely near Hamelin where Reilly's wounds were treated at a local hospital. Staff Sergeant Garrett Bartle extracted himself from his ball turret and attempted to throw the mortally wounded Oliver Gaby from the aircraft, but was unable to do so and made him comfortable in the waist of the B-17 before he left via the rear escape door.

Meanwhile on the flight deck Francis Fridgen was struggling to keep control of the gyrating aircraft since he had decided that only a crash landing would give any chance of survival to the wounded navigator and

Background photograph *The inner starboard engine has ripped off its mountings in the crash and the plexiglass nose cone has been completely smashed.*

Inset above *The tail unit of B-17 42-97474 carrying the black L in a white triangle marking of 381 Bomb Group.*

Inset right *Twisted propeller blades on the port engines indicate that both were turning when the B-17 made its final landing 5 km south of Unna at Ostendorf.*

gunner. The damaged controls eventually responded enabling the co-pilot and bombardier, Lieutenants David Waller and Phillip Palmer, to take to their parachutes, but unfortunately by this time the aircraft was too low, their parachutes failed to deploy fully and both men were killed.

Lieutenant Fridgen landed the B-17 on open ground 700 metres north-east of a small church at Stendorfer Busch, Westphalia, at approximately 14.47 hours. The aircraft broke into two pieces and according to German records was classified as being 60 per cent destroyed. Lieutenant Fridgen and Staff Sergeant Lowell Slayton, the rear gunner, discovered that Staff Sergeant Gaby had died from his wounds, but they were able to get help for Lieutenant Ehmann who was taken to the reserve hospital at Helmer. Intensive efforts by the German medical staff were not successful and the navigator succumbed to his injuries on March 8 1944.

Fire over Bucharest

The railway marshalling yards at Bucharest, designated as the target for the B-24s of the 449 Bomb Group 719 Squadron of the Fifteenth Air Force, were perfectly clear from 22,000 feet on April 4 1944, as Captain Anthony Polink lined up his aircraft, a Ford-built B-24H-10 *(42-52159)*, for its bomb run. Second Lieutenant John Zimmerman, the bombardier, hunched over his bomb-sight and passed minor corrections to Polink before announcing that his bombs were away and on target. As the B-24 turned to starboard to take up its return course which would take it back to a land fall over Brindisi, and its base at Grottaglie, the gunners warned that enemy fighters were diving on the formation. The sky was clear of cloud and visibility was unlimited, so there was no question of seeking sanctuary; the B-24s would have to fight their way out of the target area.

Polink's aircraft, which carried the number *16* on its rudders, attracted the attention of several fighters who made a head-on pass then winged over to return from the tail. The bomber was hit several times, its tail turret was set ablaze and the elevator controls shot away. Lieutenant Edward Deren, flying another 719 Squadron B-24, saw *16* slip from the formation in a right-hand spiral with smoke pouring from its No 3 engine. He watched as Polink regained control and dived the aircraft, in an attempt to put out the fire, but as he started to recover, the B-24 burst into flames and started to fall out of the sky. Deren reported that no parachutes were seen.

The tail unit of Captain Polink's B-24 showing the markings of 449 Bomb Group. The serial is in yellow and the individual number 16, in white.

The B-24 has broken in half at the point where the fire raged in the waist gun position.

Aboard the burning B-24, Staff Sergeant Clinton Wilson left his damaged rear turret and went to the waist gun positions where with the help of Staff Sergeant Angelo Bursio, he extinguished a fire in the fuselage. The two men attempted to reach their gun positions as the enemy fighters made another pass, but died instantly as a hail of cannon shells tore into the waist of the B-24. On the flight deck, Polink and his co-pilot, Second Lieutenant Paul Lahr, struggled with the controls but it became clear that there was no response from the flying surfaces, so the order to abandon the aircraft was given at 15,000 feet.

Lieutenant Zimmerman, who had been injured by a 20 mm cannon shell in the first attack, was lying semi-conscious in the nose of the aircraft, but he managed to attach his parachute to its harness and bailed out through the nose wheel doors. The ball turret and left waist gunners, Staff Sergeants John Jarrard and Edward Laver, both suffering from shrapnel injuries, left the aircraft from the waist gun positions, and Top Sergeant George Rothenburg, the top turret gunner,

went out via the bomb-bay. Rothenburg had problems with his harness and was only able to fit his parachute to one side, before the tightening turn of the B-24 told him that he would have to take his chance with his partly fitted parachute. He landed safely. Co-pilot, Lieutenant Lahr released Top Sergeant John Sickley from the nose turret then, with Captain Polink bailed out through the bomb-bay at an altitude of 500 feet. By this time the B-24 was burning fiercely in the nose and waist areas, but Rumanian peasants on the ground saw another parachute leave the aircraft after the two pilots. Just as it deployed, the B-24 spiralled into it dragging the shroud lines across its starboard wing.

Seven crew members descended safely and were treated for their wounds, but the bodies of Wilson and Buriso were found in the wreckage whilst that of the unfortunate Sickley was discovered beneath the starboard wing. All three airmen were buried in the cemetery of a small town near Cervenia next to Rumanian soldiers who had been killed in combat. The graves were attended by local people who ensured that flowers were regularly placed on them. After discharge from hospital and before being taken to a POW Camp, Lieutenant Lahr was taken to the last resting place of his colleagues and allowed to pay his last respects in solitude.

Berlin salvage

At 15.00 hours on March 6 1944, Hauptmann Voss of Airfield Headquarters 25/III Nejruppin, received a message that a B-24 bomber had crashed one mile NNW of Wall and was in a recoverable condition. Gathering a team of experts in salvage, he immediately left for the crash site which was being guarded by local volunteers.

On arrival he found that the aircraft was a Ford (Willow Run) built aircraft serial *42-7586*, and carried the markings of the 445 Bomb Group, 701 Squadron, Eighth Air Force. Dipl Ing Brunnemann, an airframes expert, reported that the aircraft had landed on one wheel and suffered 15 per cent damage. The fuselage had been twisted in the crash and parts of its upper surface as well as the starboard wing had been damaged by fire from the outer starboard engine. The tail unit was extensively damaged by bullets fired from a fighter, and there was also evidence of flak damage. While Brunnemann was examining the outside of the aircraft, Leutnant Stengele concentrated on the radio equipment, and his companion, Leutnant Blum, on the armament. The subject of their investigation was in fact the only B-24 lost that day by 445 Bomb Group. It had taken off from Tibenham as part of a force briefed to bomb the German capital and had been hit by anti-aircraft guns over the target. With one engine on fire the pilot, First Lieutenant George Lymburn, had left his place in the 'hole' position of the low formation and turned south away from the target area. The aircraft was last seen over Steglitz being harassed by an enemy fighter,

but its lowered landing gear may have convinced the German fighter pilot that the B-24 was going to attempt a landing, so he did not press home his attacks.

Lieutenant Lymburn ordered his crew to bail out which they did at an altitude of 22,000 feet. Lieutenant Sloan and Sergeant Carr left through the left waist gun position, Sergeants Bujalski and Young exited via the bomb-bay and were followed by the co-pilot, Lieutenant Roberts, whilst the navigator, Lieutenant Serpico, after releasing Sergeant Schailley from the nose turret used the nose wheel doors. The ball turret gunner, Sergeant Downey, made his escape through the camera hatch, but by the time tail gunner Sergeant Cittadino had evacuated his turret the aircraft appeared to be too low for a safe parachute descent. The tail gunner took up his crash

B-24H-1, 42-7586, one of a batch of 253 built by Ford at Willow Run. The aircraft carries the markings of 445 Bomb Group in a 6-feet diameter white circle on its fin/rudder, and a black B on a similar disc on top of the starboard wing. The serial and the code Q+ are in yellow. It is possible that the officer striding away from the group by the door, is Hauptmann Voss who was in charge of the salvage team. Note that both propellers are missing from the starboard engines, which do not, in this view, show any signs of the fire detailed in the combat and subsequent German reports.

position in the waist of the aircraft and remained there until Lieutenant Lymburn had safely landed the aircraft.

All eight parachutes were seen to open and the survivors landed in the Gruenefeld-Boernicke area where they were apprehended. Unfortunately Lieutenant Serpico landed in a field containing stumps from freshly cut-down trees, and was killed when he hit one of these, his body being recovered and given a military funeral at Schoenwalde. Hauptmann Voss' team found that the aircraft contained 4,500 rounds of unused 12.7 mm (.50 inch) machine-gun ammunition, its BC348N radio receiver was tuned to the international distress frequency, and its transmitter, type BC375E, was set at a command frequency. There was also an Ultra short-wave intercommunication set to 8,110 KCs and containing three other channels. The B-24 was stripped of all armament, radio equipment and survival gear, then transported to Neuruppin to await further instructions as to its disposal. Two of the Pratt and Whitney Twin Wasp engines were sent to an evaluation unit at Parchim, one of the main landing gear units went to the firm JFA at Dessau and two of the .50-inch calibre machine-guns together with ammunition found their way to the research centre at Rechlin.

The aircraft contained about 300 gallons of fuel which, with other components, was sent to the Technical Research Centre in Berlin. The remains of the B-24 were no doubt reduced to scrap after having removed any parts which could be used to keep similar captured aircraft, then operating with KG 200, in the air.

No doubt Voss and his team were well satisfied with their day's work, which had started at 13.45 hours over Berlin when the first shells found the vital parts of *42-7586*.

More trouble over Bucharest

While Captain Anthony Polink and his crew (see the chapter entitled 'Fire over Bucharest'), were fighting for their lives, the crew of another B-24 from the same unit was also having problems. After bombing the marshalling yards and, according to bomb aimer Second Lieutenant Adolph Ornstein, 'getting a good spread over the target', First Lieutenant John McCormick swung B-24H-5 *41-29258* away from the aiming point and headed it on to course for its base at Grottaglie.

At 20,500 feet 100 miles south-west of Bucharest, the radio operator, Top Sergeant Theodore Thompson, manning the Emmerson nose turret, called that an enemy fighter was approaching from the 12 o'clock low position. Top Sergeant Arthur Van Arkel in the top turret and Staff Sergeant Harry Dow, in the ball turret, immediately swung their guns towards the nose and all three men met the hostile fighter with a fusillade of .50-inch ammunition. The fighter passed seemingly unscathed and pulled up behind

The distinctive oval shaped fin/rudder of Lieutenant McCormick's B-24, whose drab camouflage adds a certain poignancy to the dismal scene.

the Fort Worth-built B-24 for another pass from the rear. Sergeant Dow called that his ammunition was exhausted, but said that he would track the fighter in the hope that its pilot would believe the turret was still operational. The tail and left waist gunners fired at the fighter as it bore in, raking the fuselage of the bomber from nose to tail.

Private Jesse Lowe in the right waist position, noticed that the ball turret had stopped traversing and decided to free Dow from it, but a fire broke out amidships and prevented him from reaching the turret's mechanism. Meanwhile the pilot reported that the engineer had been killed in the attack and the bombardier had also been hit. With one wing on fire and the fuselage filled with smoke, Lieutenant McCormick realised that his aircraft was beyond recovery and gave the order to bail out. McCormick and his co-pilot, Second Lieutenant Charles Lynch, fixed their parachutes and left the aircraft via the bomb-bay, whilst the waist gunners and tail gunner left through the waist gun positions.

The navigator, who was badly burned by the fire in the front of the aircraft, was last to leave via the bomb-bay, but his parachute became hooked up and the shroud lines were severed.

The B-24 was seen to spiral gently to the left and hit the ground close to the Danube near the village of Tiganesti. Five of the crew landed safely and were helped by Rumanian peasants who also recovered the bodies of their comrades from the wreck and found the remains of the navigator's parachute trapped in the bomb-bay. The five men were taken into captivity and united with Captain Polink's crew very soon after their parachute descents. No doubt the comradeship shared by the men, both in their recent frightening experiences, and in happier times on their base in Italy, helped in tempering the grief they must have all felt for their eight colleagues who had paid the ultimate price in the skies over Rumania.

Drama over Berlin

The tail unit of B-24H-1 42-7595, another Ford (Willow Run) built aircraft which was shot down during a raid on Berlin on March 8 1944. This aircraft came from 706 Bomb Squadron of 446 BG based at Bungay. It was piloted by First Lieutenant Herbert Bohnet and was attacked by fighters at approximately 14.10 hours. The aircraft was seen to catch fire when flying straight and level. Four parachutes were seen to deploy before the B24's starboard wing fell off and the aircraft spun into the ground taking the other six crew members with it. The wreckage fell in woods 6.5 km from Luckau, south of Berlin. The rear gunner, Staff Sergeant Raymond Schultz, had an amazing escape; his turret was severed from the aircraft during the attack and he freed himself from it during the descent from 20,000 feet. Two of the crew were wounded in the aircraft and both broke their legs on landing, at least two other crew members were killed during the fighter attacks which brought about the crash. Overall camouflage is olive drab, the serial and code letter E are in yellow.

Fightin' Pappy's **last fight**

October 9 1943 was a typical English autumn day, with scattered cumulus cloud dotting the pale blue sky, and the sun fighting hard to delay the onset of winter. A slight ground haze still persisted as the B-17s of 526 Bomber Squadron of 379 Bomb Group of the Eighth Air Force, left their hard standings at Kimbolton to join a force of 378 bombers briefed to attack targets at Marienburg, Gdynia, Danzig and Anklam. The previous day a large force from the 1st, 2nd and 3rd Air Division had been involved in a raid to Bremen and had been severely mauled by FW 190s from Leeuwarden and Bf 109s from Schipol, after the escorting P-47s had had to return. Despite the casualties suffered the Command still managed to raise a sizeable force whose primary targets were the FW 190 factory at Marienburg, to be attacked by 100 B-17s of the 4th and 13th Wings, and Gdynia on the Polish border which was the objective of the 40th and 45th Wings. The Arado aircraft component factory at Anklam was selected as a diversionary target and among the 115 B-17s briefed for this target was *42-5407 Fightin' Pappy*, whose pilot, First Lieutenant Vernon Smith and his crew, would be flying their fourth mission.

'*Fightin' Pappy*' was one of a batch of 2,300 B-17Fs built by Boeing at Seattle and had already completed 17 trips, the last three being in the hands of Lieutenant Smith. At 09.30 hours the eight combat wings, led by Brigadier-General Travis leading 303 Group, passed over Cromer at 1,000 feet and headed out on the first leg. The ploy to fly at low level in an attempt to foil the enemy radar was

unsuccessful, and signals picked up from the Bremen defence area indicated that the Germans were aware that a large force was approaching their airspace. Fighters were vectored into the area and as the Danish coast was approached interceptions were already taking place.

Lieutenant Smith's B-17 was flying at 11,000 feet just south of its intended course, but its formation found their target and released their bombs on time. At approximately 12.00 hours the B-17s were intercepted over Kiel by a force of FW 190s which attacked with guns and rockets. *Fightin' Pappy* was seen to leave the formation just south of Kiel and was reported to have crashed in the sea after eight men had been seen to bail out. This report turned out to be inaccurate, the crew which made it, no doubt confusing Smith's aircraft with another stricken B-17.

The aircraft had in fact spun out of the formation in the position reported, having sustained serious damage to its engines and controls. Lieutenant Smith and his co-pilot, Second Lieutenant Robert Greenhalgh, fought the spinning aeroplane's controls and managed to stop the wild gyrations, but it seemed to them that it would be wiser to stay with the aircraft and attempt a ditching in the sea rather than risk bailing out. The radio

The battered nose art of Lieutenant Smith's B-17F after it had been removed from the crash site to a dump near Kiel.

operator, Top Sergeant Johnnie Bryant, had received a cannon shell wound in the first fighter attack, but he left his gun and sent out a distress signal, then clamped the key down, and returned to his gun as more fighters were reported from the other gun positions. On the flight deck, Lieutenant Smith had managed to hold the aircraft in straight and level flight but found he was now unable to advise the crew of his intentions due to damaged intercom, so he sent the top turret gunner, Top Sergeant Joseph Lemischak, to warn them to take up their crash positions in the radio compartment. The men left their crew stations, made Sergeant Bryant as comfortable as they could, and awaited the impact. Lieutenant Smith put *Fightin' Pappy* down on a small island 15 miles north of Kiel with no further injuries to his crew.

Unfortunately the gallant Sergeant Bryant died from his wounds before the crash and his body was carried from the wreck by the navigator and bombardier, Second Lieutenants Calvin Ford and George Dickerson. The radio operator, who was recommended for a Silver Star by Lieutenant Smith, was buried with full military honours in the Post Cemetery at Kiel on November 11 1943.

Phyllis Marie joins KG 200

Assessment of the opposition is vital to any commander, and the capture of intact, or at least repairable, aircraft from opposing forces enables close study to be made of strengths, weaknesses, and suitable counter measures. In December 1942 the Luftwaffe acquired a virtually intact Boeing built B-17F when Lieutenant Paul Flickner of 303 Bomb Group landed *41-24585, Wulf Hound*, in France. The B-17 was demonstrated to fighter Gruppen and then used by KG 200 for a variety of duties which included the clandestine dropping of agents. Spares were of course a major problem, and KG 200 had to obtain these from many of the B-17s which fell victim to flak or fighters, in many cases impact with the ground made this a very difficult task. However, another complete B-17 was captured in 1943, then in 1944 a Douglas-built B-17F, *42-30713* involuntarily joined the Luftwaffe.

On March 8 1944 the USAAF mounted its second major attack on Berlin, the first having taken place the day before, and among those briefed to take part was 568 Bomb Squadron of 390 Bomb Group based at Framlingham, Norfolk. The Group lost three aircraft that day and one of them was *42-30713, Phyllis Marie* which had completed 25 missions with the 390th and nine with a previous owner.

The B-17, captained by Second Lieutenant Max Quakenbush, was part of the 'low' squadron which was heavily engaged by enemy fighters as it approached the target. At approximately 14.30 hours the bomber was seen to be straggling behind the squadron with its No 3 engine on fire, other crews watched as enemy fighters moved in for the kill, but Quakenbush lowered his undercarriage and started to lose altitude with the fighters circling at a safe distance.

It was reported by two other crews that at least eight parachutes were seen to leave the aircraft, but a further crew reported only two; in the event nine crew members were captured aboard the aircraft after the landing, the missing man being the right waist gunner, Sergeant Howard Vannoy. It seems likely therefore, that he was the only man to parachute from the B-17, although both German and USAAF records do not confirm this. Lieutenant Quakenbush and his co-pilot, Second Lieutenant Roger Johnson, successfully landed their aircraft in a field at Werben, 11 km from Cottbus, the exact position being 52-35N/14-10E. The B-17 landed with its gear down but was stopped by a drainage ditch which collapsed the port undercarriage leg.

Major Huhn of Air Field Headquarters 35/III Guben, and his team visited the site of

---

Above right *Lieutenant Quakenbush's B-17F,* Phyllis Marie, *after it came to rest in a field near Brandenburg.*

Right *The interior of the B-17 photographed by Major Huhn and his salvage team on March 8 1944.*

Far right *The tail turret of Sergeant George Schumacher, marked with nine mission symbols which are possibly those flown before it joined 390 Bomb Group. The code letter on the fin is interesting since it appears to have been changed from a C to an E.*

The mission tally showing the nine faded bombs on the bottom line which refer to operations in the hands of previous owners. The name Deadeye 750 *refers to a crew member and not the aircraft's nick name, as reported in one other publication which used this photograph. All these markings still existed during the B-17's service with KG 200.*

the crash and reported the Fortress to be only five per cent damaged. The Germans checked all the equipment aboard the B-17 and noted the frequencies being operated at the time of the combat, but they did not attempt to touch or remove any of the radio equipment which all carried bold red 'warning' signs, leading them to suspect that it was all 'booby trapped'. These fears proved to be groundless and after a bomb disposal unit had checked this, as well as the aircraft's bomb load, which was still intact, a salvage team moved in.

The B-17 had landed with all four motors running, the crew having managed to extinguish the minor fire in No 3, but on the collapse of the port undercarriage the inner port propeller was bent. It did not take long for the Luftwaffe to find a replacement, oddly enough this not coming from another B-17 but being of German manufacture and slightly smaller in diameter.

Phyllis Marie was made airworthy, her stars being replaced by crosses, and she was soon in the hands of I/KG 200 which operated her alongside another B-17F; this pair later being joined by a B-17G.

The records of KG 200 show that the B-17G, coded *A3+BB* had not been modified in any way apart from having armament removed from the ball and waist gun position and the fitting of a German airspeed indicator, a barometric altimeter, and a FuG 101 electric altimeter. All IFF and radar was also removed. This particular B-17 was lost on the night of March 2/3 1945 after dropping agents over Holland. It left Stuttgart at 23.08 hours

carrying a crew of 11, and flew on a south-westerly heading at 2,000 m, after crossing the Rhine the pilot descended to 800 m and made several course changes before carrying out his task. On the return flight the navigator became confused and took several fixes from Echterdingen but was unable to achieve clear enough responses to his requests. At 06.00 hours the aircraft was picked up by ground radar near Dijon, and shortly after was attacked and set on fire by a night fighter. The order to bail out was given but only the co-pilot, three gunners and the jump master managed to leave the aircraft. The agents carried by the B-17 on this occasion were eight men and one woman, they had been confined to the unlit interior of the aircraft's fuselage and not seen by any of the surviving crew members, the first had been dropped at 02.00 hours, and the remainder, including the woman some 20 minutes later.

At this time the commanding officer of I/KG 200 was a Major Koch who had taken over from Major Gartenfeld on his transfer to the RLM.

The prisoners taken from this B-17G

The manufacturer's detail stencilled on the port side of Phyllis Marie, *once again the name* Watford Polly *is a reference to a crew member or perhaps one of his female friends.*

reported that a B-17F, also operated by the unit, had blown up shortly after take-off from Echterdingen on an agent-dropping mission on February 10 1945.

In April 1945 troops of the US 1st Army found a B-17F of KG 200 at Altenburg, just south of Leipzig, the interior had been modified and there was evidence of bloodstains around one waist gun position, but the name *Phyllis Marie*, the mission tallies and the Swastika kill markings, still adorned the exterior; evidence of her sterling work with 390 Bomb Group which had ended near Brandenburg one year before. The wheel had turned a complete circle for one B-17, but her activities after she joined KG 200, her handling qualities with one smaller propeller, and the ultimate fate of her final Luftwaffe crew, all remain one of the secrets of World War 2, and may never be discovered.

A grounded eagle

There was nothing more comforting to the crews of the B-17s and B-24s, than the sight of their escort fighters which they affectionately called 'Little Friends'. The P-47s and P-51s shepherded their charges through hostile airspace and were always on the look out for damaged bombers trailing behind the main formations on the way home. Luftwaffe pilots learned to respect the rugged P-47s and sleek P-51s, which had sufficient range to accompany the bombers to Berlin and back. Nonetheless they still took them on in an attempt to defend their homeland, developing techniques to draw the escorts away from the bombers leaving the way clear for Bf 110s and Me 410s to tackle the lumbering Fortresses and Liberators.

4 Fighter Group was the oldest established group in the Eighth Air Force and was formed from the RAF Eagle Squadrons, hence its nick name 'The Eagles'. On September 12 1944, 334 Squadron was detailed to fly close escort to a raid on Brux/Most. The weather was hazy with $\frac{4}{10}$ cumulus cloud as the unit took off from Debden and rendezvoused with the bomber formations over the North Sea.

At 11.45 hours in the Weisbaden area Captain Thomas Joyce, leading Red Section, was advised by his number two that enemy fighters were approaching from the 4 o'clock high position. Joyce acknowledged the warning and pulled his unit into a turn to meet the hostile aircraft which turned out to be eight FW 190s. Lieutenant Rober Dickmeyer, flying as Red 3, warned Joyce that another FW 190 was coming in fast on the starboard side. The leader called his wing man's attention to the new danger and advised

him to intercept the enemy fighter whilst he (Joyce) acted as cover. Lieutenant Dickmeyer climbed away in his P-51 keeping one eye on the enemy fighters and the other on the two P-51s of his colleagues which were now diving away to the south-east heading in the general direction of Darmstadt. On return to Debden it was found that Captain Joyce, who had been flying P-51 *44-14271*, was missing. Lieutenant Dickmeyer was insistent that if the Captain had been shot down it had been by flak and not fighters. The Lieutenant's faith in his leader's ability to avoid defeat at the hands of an enemy pilot proved to be right.

At 11.58 hours at a farm 7 km south-west of Bernau, a badly damaged P-51 carried out a creditable forced landing. The pilot destroyed his gun sight and radio equipment before being apprehended by workers from the farm.

The P-51 carried the markings of 334 Fighter Squadron and the serial *414271* on its fin/rudder; one of the Eagles had been grounded.

Hauptmann Schneider of Air Field District 27/III Schoenwalde, visited the wreck and reported that the aircraft had suffered the following damage; fuselage 90 per cent, wings 60 per cent, tail unit 20 per cent and landing gear 20 per cent. The six machine-guns were removed, as was a total of 750 rounds of 12.9 mm (.50-inch) calibre machine-gun

ammunition, this was found in the wing containers, the port carrying 600 rounds and the starboard 150. All salvageable equipment, including the armament, was removed to the Luftwaffe base at Goettingen where it was evaluated by Dipl Ing Wegener, the rest of the airframe was scrapped.

Above *The P-51 of Captain Thomas Joyce of 334 Fighter Squadron after it came to rest on the farm Hobrechtsfelde near Bernau. The finish is silver overall and the band on the fin/rudder is red. Codes are in black outlined in red. The P-51 was considered by the Germans to be a 90 per cent wreck and was scrapped after equipment had been removed.*

Shady Lady

Several photographs used in this book have produced mysteries which in some cases have been solved, but in others have so far retained their secrets. One of the latter is the B-17G depicted in this set of pictures. Research over a very long period has failed to throw any light on the circumstances which resulted in this apparently undamaged aircraft being recorded by an unknown German photographer who, unfortunately, failed to get the serial into his lens.

Many records do indicate the names given by crews to their aircraft, and a B-17 of 509 Bomb Squadron, 351 Bomb Group, was called *Shady Lady*, this aircraft was a Boeing-built F model serial *42-29841* and survived the war, so it fails to meet our requirements on at least two counts.

The *3* on the port fuselage side gives a clue. Two units, 601 Bomb Squadron of 398 Bomb Group, and 832 Bomb Squadron of 486 Bomb Group, both used this number. In the first case it was followed by an *O*, and in the second by an *R*; the cut off back upright of the second letter seems to favour the letter *R*, as an *O* is more likely to have a bigger angle to its base as in the *3*. So it is possible that the code is in fact *3R*, but obviously this is only guess work. It has been suggested that the photographs were taken in Italy, if this is so then the B-17 is not likely to be an Eighth Air Force machine.

The approach of the publisher's 'deadline' for completion of this book, forced the author into deciding whether or not to include *Shady Lady*. Eventually it was decided that the pictures were too good to omit, so although at this time the B-17 still holds her secrets, she is revealed to the readers. No doubt, as is often the case in such research, a score of letters from those who did not see the original pleas for help, will come forth and tell what happened and where!

Below and following two pages *The starboard inner propeller is feathered and this is the only clue to the trouble which may have forced the B-17 down. A close examination of the three-quarter rear view of the nose, shows that the .50-inch machine-guns still have ammunition in their feeds, this also being confirmed by the nose view in which can be clearly seen the Norden Bomb Sight. Could this possibly be the B-17G used by KG 200 and mentioned in the story of Phyllis Marie?*

'Little Friends'

Above and above right *The code IV identifies this P-51 as belonging to 359 Fighter Group, 369 Fighter Squadron, Eighth Air Force based at East Wretham. Magnification of the stencil markings below the windscreen indicate serial 44-14881. It is doubtful, however, if this is in fact so, as 14881 served with 364 Fighter Group, 384 Fighter Squadron at Honington and was shot down on January 1 1945 during an escort mission to Magdeburg. The fuselage code for the 384th was 5Y. The pilot of 14881 was Second Lieutenant James Porter who was killed in the crash after combat with FW 190s, the aircraft falling at Oldendorf near Zeven at 12.05 hours. The most likely explanation is that damage to the fuselage has crumpled the markings to the extent that one of the key numbers appears incorrectly. But one must never overlook the fact that mistakes can be made in official records, as we have seen in many other cases in this book. The author's opinion is that this P-51 is not 44-14881. Ammunition from the port wing container of the P-51 can be seen above right.*

Below left and right *On the morning of November 7 1943, 13 P-47s of 355 Fighter Group, 358 Fighter Squadron, took off from Steeple Morden to escort B-17s raiding targets in France. Yellow Section comprised Captain Walter Kossack, Lieutenant John Lanphier, Lieutenant Jack Woertz and Flying Officer Chester Watson, had Second Lieutenant William Roach flying with them as a spare. Roach's aircraft was coded YF-U and carried the serial 222490 on its fin. On the way to the rendezvous Lieutenant Lanphier's aircraft developed engine trouble and he turned back, his place being taken by Roach. The bombers were late reaching the target area and this, together with unfavourable winds, left the P-47s short on fuel. The formation eventually broke up and sought the most economical way home. Lieutenant Woertz, flying No 3, advised Lieutenant Roach to follow him on a course of 355 degrees but the No 2 did not hear this advice and was last seen following the main formation.*

Lieutenant Woertz ran out of fuel near Hastings and crash-landed, but the three other pilots of Yellow Section were not so lucky and were not seen again. Two of them are believed to have landed in the Channel, but Lieutenant Roach eventually turned back and landed his P-47 near Lille. He survived the war and returned to the States in 1945. The P-47 was captured by the Luftwaffe, its cowling ring was painted yellow and Luftwaffe markings applied in place of the USAAF stars.

This page *The code QI identifies this razor-back P-47 as one operated by 356 Fighter Group, 361 Fighter Squadron which operated from Goxhill and Martlesham Heath. The unit was equipped with P-47s from September 1943 until November 1944, then switched to P-51s. Overall finish is olive drab and it is possible that the coloured segment on the wheel disc is blue. The individual aircraft letter is I and can be seen aft of the fuselage star in the picture featuring the port oleo.*

Opposite page *These three photographs depict the wreckage of two P-38Fs of 48 Fighter Squadron which operated in North Africa. One is coded ES-J but positive identification of the other is not possible for, although its serial can be seen in another photograph from the same source (41-7644), individual histories of aircraft by serials or markings are not recorded in either 14 Fighter Group or 48 Fighter Squadron records.*

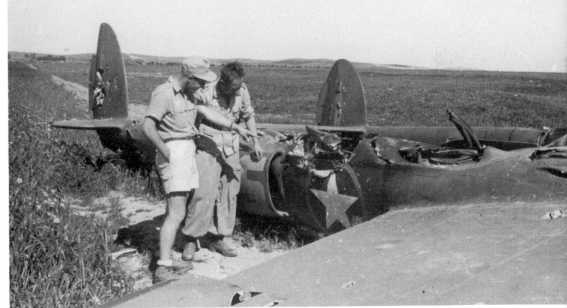

A tale of two tails

An apparently easy task can often end with a story that supports those who accept that in times of war not everyone goes by the book. This is the case with a Fifteenth Air Force B-24 which was lost over Rumania on April 4 1944. The photograph opposite clearly shows the serial *129193*, which belonged to a B-24 H-5 built by Consolidated and issued to 449 Bomber Group whose markings can also be seen. The first problem occurred when it was discovered that this particular aircraft survived the war. It was suggested that the fin had been damaged on impact and one of the letters was bent, thus giving a false reading. The photograph clearly reveals that this was not so, but the Americans were still adamant that *129193* had survived. A further check was then made of negatives on the same strip, one of these was of the same aircraft taken from the other side. Proof that this was so came not only from the fact that the negative was within three frames of the print in question, but also that the damage to the leading edge of the starboard fin, which can be seen just above the stick being carried by the rider, was also visible in the view taken from the port side. An enlargement of the photograph below revealed that the serial on the port fin was *129093*. Another search of the records brought to light that this B-24 was also operated by 449 Bomb Group and was aircraft *13*, confirmed by this number appearing on the rudder. Aircraft number *13* was a B-24H

captained by First Lieutenant Richard Kendall, and was part of a force briefed to attack Bucharest. At approximately 13.59 hours at a position 44-00N/25-15E, in clear weather the formation was attacked by several Bf 109s. The first indication Kendall had of any danger, was a call from radio operator Top Sergeant Donald Murray, who was manning the .50-inch machine-gun in his compartment. 'Fighters, 3 o'clock high', alerted the crew and immediately the gunners opened fire. A Bf 109 with guns twinkling from its wings, bore in on the B-24 and, as Murray called another warning, he was struck in the chest and died instantly. The aircraft was severely damaged and Kendall warned his crew to be ready to bail out, as he eased the Liberator from the formation. The attack started at 20,000 feet and as Kendall and his co-pilot, Second Lieutenant John Rhoades, gradually descended, the controls became stiff and the B-24 started to shudder.

At 6,000 feet the machine was virtually out of control and the order to abandon it crackled over the intercom. First to leave was the engineer, Top Sergeant Gerald Danison, who evacuated the bomber through the bomb-bay and hit the ball turret guns as he left. The co-pilot was helped from his station by Lieutenant Martin Roth, the navigator, and both left through the nose escape hatch. In the meantime there was drama in the fuselage as the injured ball and rear turret gunners attempted to escape. Both men were seriously wounded and in a shocked condition; they seemed to be unaware of the immediate

danger but were saved by the assistant engineer, Top Sergeant Warren Hollingsworth, who helped them with their parachutes then dropped the ball turret gunner out through the camera hatch, and the rear gunner through one of the waist positions. The bombardier, Lieutenant Joseph Martin, who had been helping Kendall to control the B-24, then bailed out through the nose hatch and was quickly followed by Lieutenant Kendall. The unfortunate Warren Hollingsworth, whose bravery had saved two colleagues, was unable to reach an escape hatch in time; maybe his efforts and a wound in the right foot had exhausted him too much, and his body was found in the aircraft. Hollingsworth and Murray, who had both completed 30 operations, were the only two fatal casualties. They were given a full military funeral on April 8, together with 12 other Fifteenth Air Force crewmen who had died in the same raid. Some of those who survived and were captured immediately, attended the funeral to pay their respects to their colleagues.

The solution to the mystery of the different serials is quite simple; B-24 *13* carried one serial on its starboard rudder, and a different one on its port. The probable explanation is that *129193*, which we know survived the war, was undergoing repairs when *129093* needed a new fin/rudder, so this was 'borrowed' and never returned when its temporary owner became another casualty statistic.

So those who are adamant about such matters as camouflage schemes, markings, and all ground crews always making sure that everything was just so, even in the heat of battle, should take note and hopefully learn a very common lesson from the story of *129193*, or was it *129093*?

A new paint job for *Sunshine*?

Most books about the B-24 and the USAAF Fifteenth Air Force, include at least one photograph of *'Sunshine'*, which was a Liberator operated by 716 Bomb Squadron of 449 Bomb Group from Grottaglie, Italy. The story concerning this particular aircraft, is that it landed at Venegola airport near Milan on April 9 1944, and was used by the Germans in a propaganda film which purported to show that the American crew had defected. The crew in the film were in fact Germans dressed in the flight gear of American airmen.

No excuses are made for reproducing the pictures once again, because in the opinion of the author, they are worthy of considerable study. The first task was to try and establish the identity of the B-24, initially this seemed to be easy since, with the aid of a magnifying glass, it was possible to read the serial on the fuselage stencilled under the *H* in the name. This was checked by several people who all concluded it was *42-52186*, but a check of the records indicated that the B-24 carrying this serial was in fact a Ford (Willow Run) built H-10 issued to the Eighth Air Force and shot down over Holland on May 9 1944. So it could hardly have been filmed in Italy a month before it was lost. The next step was to try as big a magnification of the print as possible, this proved nothing as the serial disappeared into the grain.

Just in case a mistake had been made, a copy of the combat report covering the loss of *52186* was obtained. This confirmed that the aircraft was a B-24H-10 and was being operated by 453 Bomb Group, 735 Bomb Squadron, when it was shot down by Bf 109s near Antwerp at 10.00 hours on May 9 1944, the pilot—who survived the combat—being Second Lieutenant Edward Perro. A further extensive examination was made of the print and this brought to light several possibilities. The second last figure still persisted in looking like an 8, but under it there was evidence of another name which could well have been interfering with the stencil marking. It was also apparent that there were several small dents in the area of the markings but the shadows cast by the sun indicated that the markings concerned were in direct sunlight and not therefore likely to be affected by an interfering shadow. It became almost certain that the B-24 had been repainted by the Germans, so the question had to be asked, 'Did they, for some reason or other, repaint the small detail stencil?' The answer would seem to be, 'very unlikely', and if they did, why select *42-52186*? Coincidence perhaps, for at that time they had no knowledge that such a B-24 existed, although working on serial blocks they may have concluded that it did.

Logically they had absolutely no reason to go to such lengths, so it must be assumed that the stencil detail is original. This being so, it throws up another anomaly, for above the serial appears the legend, *US ARMY B-24H 6 LO* the latter three characters being indistinct and could be 5 10. This does seem more likely as it is almost certain that the aircraft is *42-52106* which was a B-24H-5. So the answer looks to be that this aircraft was *106*, and either a small dent or mark on the aircraft makes the 0 appear to be 8.

There can however, be little doubt that the Liberator has been repainted. Apart from the addition of crosses over the stars, the nose art and cartoon character under the nose turret all look too clean. Look, for example, at the nose, it will be seen that there are many paint chips yet they have all conveniently missed this artwork. Similarly, the pin-up is very fresh as is the name, which shows absolutely no imperfections, an impossibility when the rest of the area on which it appears is studied carefully. The 15 bomb symbols also come into the same category, they are far too fresh to have been applied individually as each mission was completed. It is also possible to

detect traces of a previous name under the 'new' nose art, to the left of the girl and below the window the letters *PEC* can be clearly seen, and behind her right elbow a capital *J* is very evident. Finally—and this could be a case of trying entirely to convince oneself—the girl does not have the air of American style pin-ups. One could almost say that she has a Teutonic appearance, but perhaps that is going too far. The general wear and tear, the oil-splashed fuselage, the patches and chipped paintwork, all indicate that the B-24 had seen some service, and it is totally reasonable to assume that the girl, the name, the bomb symbols, and the nose number, would all have shown a similar amount of wear and tear if they had been original. The personnel in the photographs are all Germans, and it is a great pity that their colleague who wielded the camera did not get at least one good shot of the tail unit showing the serial, but perhaps that was deliberate. It is thought that the fins did carry the black triangle on a white disc of 449 Bomb Group, as well as a black *3* on a white disc and a white *5* on the rudder.

88